PRAYER DRIVEN LIFE
Daily Prayers
And Insightful Encouragements

Table Of Contents

Prayer Driven Life (Introduction)	05
Daily Prayers And Insightful Encouragements Week 01	16
Overcoming Offense	26
Daily Prayers And Insightful Encouragements Week 02	31
When God Said Speak To Me I'm Listening	41
Daily Prayers And Insightful Encouragements Week 03	46
The Challenges Of Self Discipline	56
Daily Prayers And Insightful Encouragements Week 04	62
Struggling To Forgive	72
Daily Prayers And Insightful Encouragements Week 05	78
Eight Wisdom Quotes For Motivation & Improvement	87
Daily Prayers And Insightful Encouragements Week 06	90
What Is Your Ministry?	100
Daily Prayers And Insightful Encouragements Week 07	105
Self Inflicted Wounds	115

Table Of Contents

Daily Prayers And Insightful Encouragements Week 08	120
Reposition Your Heart	130
Daily Prayers And Insightful Encouragements Week 09	135
The Importance Of Patience	145
Daily Prayers And Insightful Encouragements Week 10	149
My Journey To Overcome Depression	159
Daily Prayers And Insightful Encouragements Week 11	164
Realigning My Behavior Improved My Finances	174
Daily Prayers And Insightful Encouragements 12	180

Daily Devotional Scriptures

Isaiah 26:3
2 Corinthians 12:6
Psalms 91:1-16
Psalms 34:18
Psalms 147:3
Psalms 32:8
Hebrews 4:16
2 Corinthians 12:9
Isaiah 54:10
Romans 12:12
Romans 8:24:25
Colossians 3:2
Romans 12:2
Isaiah 26:23
John 15:5
Proverbs 12:22
Proverbs 6:16-19
Romans 8:5-6
2 Timothy 1:7
Psalms 41:3
Isaiah 41:10
Philippians 4:7
Matthew 5:4
Psalm 34:18
Philippians 2:12-13
1 John 1:7-9

James 5:14-16
1 John 4:8
James 4:7,
Ephesians 6:11
James 1:5 says
Proverbs 16:9
Psalm 32:8
Psalm 37:23,
Philippians 4:6-7
Isaiah 26:3-4
Proverbs 3:5-6
Romans 12:1-2
Matthew 16:24
2 Corinthians 6:14
Matthew 12:36
Proverbs 18:21
Colossians 4:6
Romans 8:25
2 Timothy 1:7
Psalms 41:3
Isaiah 41:10
Philippians 4:7
Matthew 5:4
Psalm 34:18
Romans 6:16-20
Luke 22:42

This book contains Scripture taken from the New King James Version®. Copyright © 1982 by Thomas Nelson. Used by permission. All rights reserved.

Chapter 01
PRAYER DRIVEN LIFE
"A Foundation Built On Prayer"

INTRODUCTION

Hello! My name is Roland Gaskin Sr., and I thank you for reading my new book, "PRAYER DRIVEN LIFE." This book consists of daily prayers, inspirations, and personal insights. This book will encourage, inspire, and motivate you to live a prosperous, fulfilling life. Throughout my life, I've had my share of challenges, and I'm genuinely grateful to be able to share what God has inspired me to write over the years.

"Prayer has its way of altering one's thoughts and keeping one's mind focused on what's most important in life, which should always be GOD our Father."

I started writing prayers and inspirational messages each morning to help channel my focus. It was also a way to maintain a positive perspective on life each day. The content in this book has inspired me throughout my life, and it has helped me to develop a consistent prayer life. *Prayer has its way of altering one's thoughts and keeping one's mind focused on what's most important in life, which should always be GOD our Father*

When I decided to take on social media challenges, I realized from reading many social media posts that people often experience the same things I've experienced throughout my life. I'm Grateful God has giving me the wisdom to release encouraging words and impactful prayers on social media. Motivating myself and inspiring others has been my life's passion, and I'm truly blessed and grateful that God continues to pour much-needed wisdom into me. His guidance motivates me to consistently post positive messages on social media to inspire many people.

"Life is not complicated, but we make it difficult when we fail to apply His principles daily.

I strongly believe in discipline, and I'm grateful God has helped me to stay humble so that I do not become rebellious toward discipline. I've learned throughout my life how important it is to be humble and always show compassion towards others while keeping love in my heart because I know God is love, and love is what He has consistently demonstrated toward us. God truly loves us, and we should always love as He loves. *1 John 4:8 says, "Anyone who does not love does not know God because God is love."*

PRAYER IS A DRIVEN FORCE

I've always believed that to live life successfully, you must pray daily. Life requires patience, which has always helped me become more disciplined. Discipline helps us to live life without complications. When I think about the phrase "Prayer Driven Life," it's about establishing a relationship with God through prayer and consistently communicating with Him. It's about seeking guidance and wisdom so that I can effectively navigate through life each day. As it is written in *James 1:5, "If any of you lacks wisdom, let him ask God, who gives generously to all without reproach, and it will be given him."*

So often, we live life as if it is complicated, clearly not understanding that God has already established basic principles through His words to help us live a fulfilling and fruitful life. Life is not complicated, but we make it difficult when we fail to apply His principles daily. If we understand the process of kingdom living and implement God's principles consistently, we have a greater understanding of how to fulfill God's purpose for our lives. This is why we must stay rooted in knowledge, seeking God daily to gain wisdom through His words. We must read and meditate on God's words and make it our daily routine. We must also extract as much as we can when we study and apply His principles to our lives to experience the joy of fruitful living.

PRAYER: THE ROOT OF MY FOUNDATION

I spent my entire childhood living with my Grandmother, Lucille Gaskin (aka Mrs Lucy). I was raised in a small city called Ocilla, GA, and it was my Grandmother who took on the responsibility of raising me from birth. At the same time, my mother, Evangelist Lavonne Gaskin, left the city of Ocilla and went to New Jersey to find work to make a better life for herself and support me and my siblings. My childhood was such a blessing, knowing I had the kind of love and support from two of the most amazing women I've ever known. My mother provided the best financial support to assist my Grandmother as she raised her kids. I can't recall a day of my life ever having to lack for anything as a child. Because of their untiring love and support, I will always be grateful for their love and sacrifices.

The memories I treasure the most from my childhood are the times I spent living with my Grandmother. I remember how she used to sit quietly in her room before retiring to bed, spending hours reading her Bible out loud and praying. Praying and reading her Bible was my Grandmother's daily routine. It was something she did consistently for as long as I could remember. I couldn't imagine myself being as consistent as she was when I was younger. She would often read the Bible every night, and even today, I find myself still amazed at how consistent she was, constantly reading her Bible and praying daily. When my Grandmother passed, she was found sitting in her living room holding her Bible, which she was reading just seconds before she passed. Even to this day, as I sit quietly, it feels as if I can hear her voice praying and reading out loud. Oh, how I would give anything to listen to the sound of her voice right now. As a child, I didn't appreciate the presence of her voice as much as I do now. Since I'm older, I understand how important prayer is in my life. Prayer helps us to develop a relationship with God. It requires a commitment and it also requires one to make sacrifices to establish a consistent relationship with God.

My Grandmother didn't have much of a life. She often stayed home most of the time, devoting her life to raising her grandkids. It was the kind of sacrifice many grandmothers make in this generation. My Grandmother's foundation was always prayer. Prayer was the pillar of her life, and by laboring in prayer, she has sown seeds that are constantly manifesting in my life even today.

SURROUNDED BY A GENERATION OF PRAYER WARRIORS

Looking further into my childhood, I couldn't finish this chapter without mentioning my great grandfather Cornelius Anderson, also known to many in the community as Mr. Yank Anderson. Papa was the pillar of prayer in my hometown of Ocilla, Georgia. Compared to my Grandmother, he was like a prayer warrior on steroids. He would spend countless hours sitting on an old, rugged bench in front of his garden, praying and talking to God from sun up to sun down. People in my home town would often tease me because they said I looked and walked precisely like Papa. There wasn't a day when I would go by his house to take his daily meals, which my Grandmother had prepared for him; he wouldn't be sitting on this old rugged bench staring out at his garden, praying out loud, and talking to God. So often, I would sit beside him and listen to him pray, unbothered by my presence; he never ceased praying to acknowledge me or even acknowledge that I had brought his daily meal. He just kept praying, sticking to his daily prayer routine. As Papa often prayed, he would hold my hand, griping them tightly, staring ahead towards his garden, speaking in tongues, and praying without ceasing. Even today, as I reminisce on his life, I can still feel those grips of his hand, holding my hands tightly as his prayers became more intense.

I learned so much about the importance of prayer, being surrounded by grandparents who prayed so often. Even to this day, I've benefited from their prayers, and it's a blessing to know that such powerful prayers have stood the test of time. It's also proof that God's word is power, and prayer keeps us on a solid foundation. Prayer strengthens our faith, and faith pleases God; it also positions us to trust Him with our lives, no matter how difficult things might seem.

ESTABLISHING MY FOUNDATION FOR PRAYER

Patience is essential when it comes to prayer, and having a lack of patience as you pray can be ineffective for several reasons. First, impatience causes frustration, especially when looking for instant results. It's important to understand that prayers are not always answered the very moment we pray because everything happens in God's timing; therefore, the manifestation of our prayers will come to pass in His set timing. And secondly, God doesn't move because we're impatient. Indeed, He knows what we need and He knows what we're going through, so having faith as we pray helps us develop an effective prayer life. ***Hebrews 11:6 says, " But without faith it is impossible to please Him, for he who comes to God must believe that He is, and that He is a rewarder of those who diligently seek Him."***
I'm so grateful to reap the benefits of my grandparents and my mother's prayers. Their faith and commitment to prayer have played an essential part in shaping my life into who I am today.

Unlike my Grandmother, my mother wasn't quite as patient with letting me choose my direction; in many ways, it created a wedge in our relationship, which I've always regretted. After my grandmother's passing, my mother and I grew closer and found common ground in our relationship. In a way, spiritual maturity played a big part in helping me to change my perceptions about my mother. I finally realized I was more like my mother than I cared to admit. She was always the one person who believed that there was a calling upon my life to preach the gospel or to motivate people and draw them near to God. She would constantly pray for me and pray that God would get me on the right path to preach the gospel. We would always talk about it, but it wasn't until two days before her death, after talking with her on the telephone, that it finally resonated in my mind what she had confessed and believed was to be true. "Someday, God will use you mightily, she said to me that day. And I asked her, "How do you know?" And she replied, "Because this has been my prayer for many years, and I genuinely believe that one day God will answer those prayers." After hanging up the telephone that day, my spirit felt differently; it was as if God Himself was speaking through my mom. So often, we expect to hear from God directly, but when you truly learn to know God's heart, you can hear him even as people are speaking to you, their words are confirmation that He has already placed in your heart. After speaking with my mom, I couldn't help but think how the effectual prayers of these two incredible women, my grandmother, and mother, had shaped my destiny and put me on the right path to being who God called me to be.

Several years after the death of my mother and after my grandmother had long passed, I felt this feeling of emptiness, which I'd never really felt in my life before. At first, I assumed it was because I was still grieving their loss, but for the life of it, I couldn't understand this feeling and why it felt so overwhelming. It was a feeling of emptiness, almost to the point that depression started to come upon me. I couldn't imagine the loss of a loved one would cause me to grieve for so long, but it was an overwhelming feeling that took over my ability to think straight.

"One can never truly be prepared for death, but through God's grace and healing, He quickly restores us from our sorrows."

As time passed, It became more of a struggle mentally trying to deal with losing my parents. It was as if God's hands were released from my life. Imagine how awful that feels. I realized I needed to overcome this feeling, so I decided my best course of action was to gravitate toward the one thing I knew that never failed me: to seek God in prayer. After my parents died, I didn't feel like praying as much. I felt as if God had taken away the very ones I depended on to pray for me and be there for me when I needed someone to talk to. This is the one thing the enemy wants to see in all of us because he knows that if he can keep us caught up in our emotions, we can quickly become distracted from praying and seeking God. Being caught up in my feelings is what kept me overwhelmed in sorrow. It kept me distracted and caused me to lose my desire to pray, meditate, and seek God consistently. Even as I struggle to overcome my grief, I never really lost the concept of how powerful prayer is; it's always been my foundation throughout my life, especially when dealing with things beyond my control.

So often, I would spend countless nights crying out to God, desperately hoping to hear from him, hoping to get rid of this feeling of emptiness that was upon me, but as time passed, depression started to take its grip on me. Almost three weeks had passed, yet there were still no answers to my prayers. The one thing I learned most about God is that He doesn't move because we're desperate, but faith moves God. Therefore, I was determined to keep my faith and not give up.

Early one Tuesday morning around 5:00 AM, a sweet and pleasant voice awakened me, saying, "Get up! Shaken by the voice I heard, I nervously stood up in bed, only to realize I was the only one in the room. The voice commanded me once more; "Get up and pray for a while," it said. So, I immediately knew the Holy Spirit was speaking to me because this voice gave me a renewed feeling of peace. It was the kind of peace I felt when

I heard my Grandmother praying at night. So, without hesitation, I immediately got up and started praying. I prayed for nearly an hour until I could no longer feel the presence of the Holy Spirit in the room. It was without any warning the presence of His Spirit vanished, but His peace stayed within me for quite some time afterward, and it delivered me from depression.

After such a beautiful encounter, I continued to awaken each morning, praying and seeking God for wisdom. Hoping to feel His presence again, but He never returned for quite some time afterward. I continued to obey the instructions I was given by the Holy Spirit, waking up consistently each morning, praying, and meditating on His words daily. The one thing I learned from my Grandmother is the importance of consistency in everything you do. Consistency brings results; this is why many of us often fail with prayer. We must always be consistent in seeking God, even if we don't feel his presence or see the results we're seeking right away; you have to consistently pray, seeking God daily, staying steadfast in His word. Our lives have so much peace when we pray and trust God.

When I feel the presence of the Holy Spirit and the peace of God upon my life, I no longer feel emptiness, and I'm no longer overwhelmed by life's challenges. I desire always to pray and seek God more and more each day. I realized why I had so much emptiness inside after I developed a routine of praying and communicating with God. God revealed to me how for many years I depended so much on my grandmother and mother's prayers as the source of my relationship with Him. Still, after their passing, instead of me continuing as they had done consistently for many years, I created this distance between Him and I. God revealed to me that he allowed me to be consumed with such feelings of emptiness so that it would put me in a place of needing Him, He also did it so that it would cause me to draw near to Him. When I began to establish my relationship with God, this is when I drew closer to Him. God said, "My grieving is no excuse for not being committed to Him." He also said death is a process of life. Therefore, I must never let sorrow overwhelm me, but I should always focus on fulfilling His purpose and preparing for eternal life with Him. There's a greater need to sacrifice more of myself to stay connected to God, staying obedient to His will while continuing to labor in His words daily and developing my foundation of a **prayer-driven life.**

I thank God for conditioning me to write and share this book with others. Being inspired by my Grandmother, who labored in prayer on my behalf for many years, has helped me build a solid foundation based on the power of prayer. ***PRAYER IS POWER***, and it helps us stay connected to God daily. I enjoy sharing the many prayers God has inspired me to write and post daily on my social media platforms. It has allowed me to be a blessing to others and become resourceful, encouraging those trying to find peace daily. Life consumes so much of our time, and it's often challenging as well, but I hope there's something in this book to help you along your life's journey each day. As I always say, "Keep Life Simple" without making the process difficult.

I pray that you enjoy these simple yet powerful prayers and insights and read them as often as you desire, hoping that they will encourage your life daily. There is nothing complicated about praying, and even the simplest prayer is powerful and effective if it accomplishes its task of enhancing your life and bringing you closer to God, our Father, blessings to all of you.

"It's important always to find peaceful ways to address any situation, and with God's guidance, you will always respond positively.
#PrayerDrivenLife

DAILY PRAYERS
AND INSIGHTFUL ENCOURAGEMENTS
WEEK 01

Monday

SCRIPTURE:
Isaiah 26:3
You will keep in perfect peace those whose minds are steadfast, because they trust in you.

Heavenly Father, above all things, today, I am grateful for life and wisdom. For it is You who have given me reasons to smile through all of life's struggles. Please help me be patient with myself as you continue to nurture, repair, and restore me to a place of peace and humbleness. Every day is challenging, but because of Your grace upon my life, these challenges are just obstacles I can overcome. Your words say in ***Isaiah 26:3, "You will keep him in perfect peace, Whose mind is stayed on You, Because he trusts in You"*** It is these words, Father God, which is my hope, my shield; it keeps me far away from my distractors. In Jesus name, I pray, Amen.

Tuesday

Be Original

Be original, but don't alter yourself to be something or someone you're not. There is beauty in each of us; inside of you is a beautiful person, but you must learn to appreciate the beauty of who God made you to be without altering yourself. There's nothing more significant than self-love. There's nothing more powerful than loving yourself unconditionally and having confidence, knowing that if anyone else doesn't love me, I will love me to the fullest. You don't t have to convince the world that you are beautiful. When you feel amazing and know within yourself that you are an amazing person, no opinion is powerful enough to alter your perception of yourself. Yes, I am amazing! Yes, I am beautiful! Yes, I truly love me with all my heart! That's should be your confidence every day!!!!

SCRIPTURE:
1 Peter 3:3-4
Your beauty should not come from outward adornment, such as elaborate hairstyles and the wearing of gold jewelry or fine clothes. 4 Rather, it should be that of your inner self, the unfading beauty of a gentle and quiet spirit, which is of great worth in God's sight.

Wednesday

SCRIPTURE:

Isaiah 26:3
You will keep in perfect peace those whose minds are steadfast, because they trust in you.

Lord Jesus, help me to always love each day with a forgiving heart and a spirit without judgment. Every day, I strive to walk as You, Lord, to be of good character, show compassion for those in need, and be kind to those who are unkind, with hopes that Your glory in me brings about change in others. Lord, I pray for my family and my friends. I pray for those who have lost their way. Help me, Lord, to find strength within myself in a world that constantly tests my patience and is often so demanding. Every day, I need Your guidance; I depend on Your words to empower my thinking and restore my heart to peace. *Isaiah 26:3 says, "You will keep him in perfect peace, Whose mind is stayed on You, Because he trusts in You." I Trust You* **Lord**, *In Every Area Of My Life.* In Jesus name, I pray, Amen.

"Sometimes God moves us in ways we cannot comprehend, but often times we move too quickly causing the most confusion .
#PrayerDrivenLife

Thursday

Facing Your Truth

One of my greatest weaknesses throughout my life was hearing the truth about myself. I was comfortable with you as long as you were satisfied with who I am, but sometimes, we need someone who loves us enough to tell us the truth. Sometimes, facing the truth about yourself can be difficult to accept. Seeing your flaws is easier when you're open-minded to corrections. I'm thankful God has positioned my heart to listen without "rejected hearing." Wisdom has taught me to absorb "effective criticism" and use it to change my life when necessary. It is wise to refrain from rejecting change or self-improvement. Learn to analyze and critique yourself, and most importantly, learn to face reality and realize that we are all a work in progress, but with God's help and guidance, victory will surely be the outcome.

SCRIPTURE:

James 3:2 (NIV®)
We all stumble in many ways. Anyone who is never at fault in what they say is perfect, able to keep their whole body in check.

Friday

SCRIPTURE:
Psalms 91:1-16

He who dwells in the secret place of the Most High Shall abide under the shadow of the Almighty. 2 I will say of the Lord, "He is my refuge and my fortress; My God, in Him I will trust."

Father, in the name of Jesus, I pray for mental stability and the renewal of minds and souls throughout this nation. People have become so incompetent in their thinking, so vulnerable in their hearing, and so easily influenced that it has affected the behavior of many. We need prayer as well as sound biblical teaching in this society more than ever, Father God, and we need a call for disciples to rise up, boldly speaking your words throughout this land. I pray for those who are committed to serving Your purpose; I pray for prayer warriors who are constantly under attack, that You shall sustain them and keep them under Your protection, free from any distractions. We need love and unity; we need protection for our kids who suffer at the hands of heartless-minded people. Our faith is in You, Father God, and I continue to believe with faith your presence is always upon us. *Psalms 91:1-16 says,* **"He who dwells in the secret place of the Most High Shall abide under the shadow of the Almighty. I will say of the Lord, "He is my refuge and my fortress; My God, in Him I will trust." Surely He shall deliver you from the snare of the fowler And from the perilous pestilence. He shall cover you with His feathers, And under His wings you shall take refuge; His truth shall be your shield and buckler. You shall not be afraid of the terror by night, Nor of the arrow that flies by day."** In Jesus name, I pray, Amen.

Saturday

Point To Myself

If I keep my hand pointed in a U-turn position, I will always stay focus on God and keep my focus on improving myself instead of focusing on others. What good is it to magnify other people's faults and never address my own? Every day is an opportunity to develop a better me. There is so much in me that needs improvement until I don't have time to criticize anyone else. Learning who God desires you to be is essential because we often spend so much of our energy worrying about what people are doing and how they live their lives. When it comes to me as an individual, this is irrelevant. I have a responsibility to myself to be the best Me I can be, and that my friend is the most challenging part of my life. But with God's help and discipline, I shall succeed.

SCRIPTURE:
Romans 8:9 (NIV®)
But you are not in the flesh but in the Spirit, if indeed the Spirit of God dwells in you. Now if anyone does not have the Spirit of Christ, he is not His.

Sunday

SCRIPTURE:
Psalms 34:18, Psalms 147:3
The Lord is near to those who have a broken heart, And saves such as have a contrite spirit.

God understands everything we go through, even when our hearts feel broken. Yes, I know you might be hurting. I understand that your emotions might be getting the best of you, but you must trust God and know He is God through good times and bad times. Whoever needs this message today, I release this prayer in your situation. Pray this prayer with me . . .

Heavenly Father, restore me to a place of peace and lift this heavy burden from my heart today. Strengthen me, Father God, and help me see beyond the pain in my heart. Above all things, I trust You; my faith is in You, Father God, to see me through these difficult times. Your words say in **Psalms 34:18, "The Lord is near to those who have a broken heart, And saves such as have a contrite spirit."** And **Psalms 147:3 says, "He heals the brokenhearted And binds up their wounds."** Therefore, I trust and believe that healing shall come forth. A renewed strength shall rise in me, bringing comfort and joy to my soul. In Jesus name, I pray Amen

"Sometimes we waste so much time trying to change people. Maybe they don't need to change. Maybe you need to change the way you view them, or maybe you just need to mind your own business and work on yourself

#PrayerDrivenLife

Chapter 02
OVERCOMING OFFENSE

FOOTNOTE

One of the most extraordinary *things you can learn is dealing with offense.* Often, *it's best to remain quiet* rather *than allow any offense you might encounter to drive you into emotional responses, which can easily cause one to act out of character. The devil knows if he can lure you into operating out of your emotions, he can control your responses to offense. The word says in* **James 1:19, "So then, my beloved brethren, let every man be swift to hear, slow to speak, slow to wrath;"** *Also, Jesus said to His disciples in* **Luke 17:1** *that offense will come. Therefore, learning to deal with offense swiftly stops the devil in his tracks. The more you* fuel *the fire with your responses, the greater the power you give to the offender.*

OVERCOMING OFFENSE

It's incredible how easily it is for us to get off track when we experience offense. We become more tolerant of offense when it happens to someone else until we get offended. I remember some time ago at one of my former places of employment, there always seemed to be tension and chaos between my supervisor and my coworkers, but he really wasn't a problem for me, and quite frankly, he and I never had any negativity between us. On the other hand, my coworkers often complained about our supervisor's attitude and treatment towards them. Still, I never needed to invoke myself into their situation because I had a different experience than they had with him.

"Offense can be a powerful hindrance that **unexpectedly alters** one's *position, perception, and views."*

Early one morning, just as I arrived at work, I found myself on the other side of the fence of offense, as my supervisor, whom I had never had an issue with before, suddenly turned against me because I would not support his behavior as his superiors were questioning him concerning his behavior towards their employees. It was because of my statement against his behavior his manager reprimanded him, and that didn't sit well with my supervisor because he expected me to lie about the situation. Still, I certainly couldn't do that because his behavior towards the people he supervised warranted the discipline he was to face.

For several weeks, his attitude towards me changed drastically. He constantly tried to micromanage my duties at work, which often frustrated me, and my frustration caused me to lash out at him, which was beneath my character. I couldn't help but think how amazing and calm one can be in a hostile environment when it's not affecting them, but when you see yourself facing the same situation, how quickly you revert from being the calm one amid chaos and act the same as those who are engaging in emotional outbursts.

I arrived for work earlier than usual on Tuesday morning to meditate and pray, sitting alone in the parking lot before my shift began. While praying, the Holy Spirit asked me, "Have you yet to learn from your advice? Quite puzzled by the question, I asked the Holy Spirit, "What advice are you referring to?" Then, the Holy Spirit reminded me how I used to speak to many of my coworkers about how they should respond to offense, yet my response to offense was just as bad as theirs. He told me how their responses quickly justified their behaviors toward offense because my response was the same as theirs. He told me that if I wanted people to listen to my advice, I must be a better example, and my responses must differ."

After the Holy Spirit ministered to me, I immediately knew I had to handle the situation with my supervisor differently. So, I meditated on ***James 1:19 and Luke 17:1*** until my spirit had a sense of peace and calmness. Immediately when I walked into the building, my supervisor directed his attitude towards me, but this time, I didn't respond negatively. I just listened to what he had to say and went about my assignments for that day. It appeared that my silence aggravated him even worse. Yet, my response was very polite and calm, which didn't seem to set well with him, so suddenly, out of nowhere, he began to go off on one of his tantrums, totally shouting abusive words, as I ignored him. By then, his boss entered the room, shocked by what he was hearing. He intervened quickly and immediately escorted him to his office. I knew my supervisor was about to be terminated, so I rushed to his manager's office and pleaded with him not to fire my supervisor because I knew how badly he needed his job. I asked the manager to allow us to settle our differences, and I must admit, he and his manager were quite surprised by my request. The manager decided to try it for a while but warned him that termination would be the following action if he didn't change his behavior towards company employees.

After hearing about how I saved my supervisor's job, my coworkers seemed quite disappointed. They were puzzled that I would fight for the supervisor's job, especially after he was rude. Still, my actions changed the atmosphere in the room. The supervisor apologized, and his attitude and behavior changed immediately. He seemed humble after the encounter, but my response to offenses set in motion the much-needed change in our environment. We all learned so much from that experience. It taught me how to deal with offensive encounters. It also helped me to realize how powerful silence can be in certain situations. Often, it's better to remain calm than to respond aggressively. We often allow our emotions to trigger our reaction, but the most effective response toward offense is to be slow and cautious until God gives you peace to deal with it. Yes, sometimes there are situations when you have to stand up for yourself, but there's a way to do things, and sometimes it's best to control your emotions before you try to manage the situation.

DAILY PRAYERS
AND INSIGHTFUL ENCOURAGEMENTS
WEEK 02

Monday

SCRIPTURE:
Corinthians 12:9
And He said to me, "My grace is sufficient for you, for My strength is made perfect in weakness." Therefore most gladly I will rather boast in my infirmities, that the power of Christ may rest upon me.

The most beautiful thing you can do today is smile. Even if you don't feel like it, smile anyway. So often, we allow life to overwhelm us. We give in to it as if it's the driving force that controls our mood each day. Do you not know the power you possess? Do you not know who you are and whom you belong to? Let's pray this prayer together . . .

Heavenly Father, my confidence is in Your words daily, knowing that You control everything concerning my life. **Hebrews 4:16 says, "Let us therefore come boldly to the throne of grace, that we may obtain mercy and find grace to help in time of need."** And **2 Corinthians 12:9 says, "My grace is sufficient for you, for My strength is made perfect in weakness."** Therefore I will boast all the more gladly of my weaknesses, so that the power of Christ may rest upon me." Thank You, Father God, for the assurances of Your words each day. I'm truly grateful for Your unconditionally love. In Jesus name, I pray, Amen.

Tuesday

Rejecting Liars

Many people constantly try to convince us that lying is ok, but it's not ok. It's a sin to lie, and to do it freely and do it all the time is despicable. Who amongst us can trust a liar to tell the truth? To lie is to mislead. Lying does not represent who the Lord is, and those who try to convince you otherwise genuinely don't know God. Just look at ***Proverbs 6:16-19 and 12:22***, which clearly state that "Lying lips are an abomination to the Lord." It does not say it's acceptable to lie for any reason. How can one be a leader, lead a congregation, or represent God in any manner, and not condemn lies or not hold those who tell them accountable?

Don't allow the "INFLUENCES" of this world to cause you to be acceptable to something God is totally against. Guard your hearts, Saints! Satan has "INFLUENCES" in places and with people whom you least expect!!

Wednesday

SCRIPTURE:
Isaiah 54:10, Isaiah 26:3
For the mountains shall depart And the hills be removed, But My kindness shall not depart from you, Nor shall My covenant of peace be removed," Says the Lord, who has mercy on you.

Heavenly Father, I pray for this nation, for the minds of so many who are misguided by influence and deceptions. We are in the last days where evil has taken grip in this world, but there is hope knowing that You are our God above all things, and no weapons designed to destroy us shall prosper. Your word says in ***Isaiah 26:3, "You will keep him in perfect peace, Whose mind is stayed on You, Because he trusts in You." Isaiah 54:10 tells us that "For the mountains shall depart And the hills be removed, But My kindness shall not depart from you, Nor shall My covenant of peace be removed,"*** Says the Lord, who has mercy on you. This is the confidence we have daily to put our trust in You Lord God. To know that in Your words we shall find comfort, and know Your heart as well as Your ways, and not be influenced or misguided by evil spirits which live amongst us. In Jesus name I pray for us all. Amen.

"Entertaining a lot of people with your anger does not help your situation, instead, it can attract unhealthy attention to your problems, but prayer and meditation, helps you to gain much needed wisdom from God on how to best deal with your situation"

#PrayerDrivenLife

Thursday

Being About Your Purpose

At some point in your life, you must know your purpose and allow that to be your driven focus. Everyone has goals they are trying to fulfill, but what about YOU? What about your goals? What about your purpose? If you genuinely want to find out how much people value you, then focus on yourself for a change; become so busy with yourself, so much to the point that you're too busy to be bothered by anyone else. I learned to say no, or to simply say I don't have time, because I'm too busy trying to fulfill my purpose and goals. Remember, if you genuinely want to be successful, you must prioritize Yourself. You must understand the gifts within you and spend every day **nurturing**, **developing**, and **investing** in yourself. Learn to put value to your skillsets. REMEMBER THIS: If you don't charge people what you're worth, they will pay someone else what you're worth. Everyone is trying to achieve something in life, so it's important for you to always strives to reach that next level for yourself. Still, if you genuinely want to achieve greatness, you must become selfish and be driven by your purpose. I encourage you to work towards excellence, invest in yourself, empower yourself with education and training, and, most importantly, develop consistency that keeps you driven and focused on your purpose.

Friday

SCRIPTURE:
Colossians 3:2
Set your mind on things above, not on things on the earth.

Romans 12:2
And do not be conformed to this world, but be transformed by the renewing of your mind, that you may prove what is that good and acceptable and perfect will of God.

Heavenly Father to sustain myself each day, I must equip and empower my mind to stay focused on those things which are above. Your words say in **Colossians 3:2 to** "Set your mind on things above, not on things on the earth" And **Romans 12:2 it says " And do not be conformed to this world, but be transformed by the renewing of your mind, that you may prove what is that good and acceptable and perfect will of God."** Help me Father God, sustain me with guidance and wisdom to approach each day in an effective and positive way, while keeping my mind at peace. In Jesus name I pray, Amen.

Saturday

Striving For Greatness

Many times, we live so much of our lives being comfortable with who we are, not realizing that tapping into your potential is something you must strive for every day. How can you even grow if you never look beyond yourself? How can you achieve greatness without working towards excellence or taking advantage of opportunities that come your way and trusting that God is opening doors for you to walk through? Each one of us has an economy inside of us. We have the potential to sustain ourselves if we genuinely labor to harbor our gifts, but bringing out the best of who you are only happens with knowledge and investment. It requires as much time as possible to hone our skills and tap into resources that help us empower ourselves through knowledge. It's incredible how often people come to me seeking help with their ideals without even having the slightest plan about what they are trying to accomplish, nevertheless having a vision. This is not preparation; it often only amounts to failure, or you give up altogether.

If you genuinely have a desire to reach greatness. Always know that greatness requires **SACRIFICE**, greatness requires **KNOWLEDGE**, greatness requires **CONSISTENCY**, greatness requires **INVESTMENT**, and most importantly, greatness requires **FAITH**. Don't just live your life; live it every day striving to achieve excellence!!

Sunday

SCRIPTURE:
John 15:5
"I am the vine, you *are* the branches. He who abides in Me, and I in him, bears much fruit; for without Me you can donothing.

Heavenly Father, my desire is to have stability through Your words each day to know that no matter how difficult the world becomes, no amount of difficulties can move me. Your word says in ***John 15:5, "I am the vine, you are the branches. He who abides in Me, and I in him, bears much fruit; for without Me you can do nothing.".*** You are my strength Father God and my shield, You prune me so that I may bear more fruit, I am clean because of the words You have spoken to me. Apart from You, Father God I am nothing, and I can do nothing. Without You there is no direction or path. Help me to live a disciplined life Father, and restore in me a clean heart with hopes that I may live each day pleasing you. In Jesus name, I pray Amen

"Add WISDOM to your diet daily. The more you eat, the wiser you become."
#PrayerDrivenLife

Chapter 03

THAT MOMENT WHEN GOD SAID; "SPEAK TO ME, I'M LISTENING"

1 John 5:15
And if we know that he hears us in whatever we ask, we know that we have the requests that we have asked of him.

PRAYER

Heavenly Father, create in me the right spirit, the right mindset, not to be influenced by the things of this world, but having a mind that rejects sin, a mind that hunger for knowledge and righteousness. Thank You, Father, for Your words each day, for guidance and understanding, and also for the conviction your words bring, which keeps my heart pure. Assist me, Father God in developing a relationship with the Holy Spirit. Thank You for correction and discipline, which keeps me in line with You. I desire to always live my life pleasing to You, Father, to never compromise righteousness for sin, but to know Your truth, and to live it with all sincerity in my heart each day, for this I cannot accomplish without a commitment to You, in Jesus name I pray Amen.
Romans:6:13,

SPEAK TO ME. I'M LISTENING

In the early years of my life, at the age of 12, I began to gravitate towards church, and I must admit, I was overwhelmed trying to figure out my purpose for being there. I understood God's calling for my life, but I didn't understand how to pursue it. I used to think that there were specific ways I needed to pray and communicate with God to establish a close relationship with Him. I often sought advice from pastors, or I would constantly watch people as they were praying, clearly not understanding that other people's communication with him should not determine my relationship with God.

Still, it's about my conversations and relationship with Him, praying and speaking sincerely from my heart.

As I look back on my beginnings and approach to prayer, I still can't believe how complicated most of the answers I received from pastors about how we should pray. I recalled many times walking away from conversations with pastors after giving me advice about how I should pray. Those conversations often left me feeling confused and frustrated. It had me feeling that prayer was such a complicated task. It's puzzling how people who are supposed to be mature in Christ can easily misinterpret God's word. I also felt ignorant trying to adapt to many different methods of praying, mostly imitating what I saw from others as they were praying, and because of that, I wasn't getting results. I was certainly trying too hard to talk to God, and it wasn't sincere from my heart. I felt pressured, not realizing I needed to speak to God from my heart.

Early one Monday morning, I eagerly awakened, ready to begin my daily meditation and prayer routine, but as usual, I found myself struggling while praying. It felt as if my prayers didn't reflect what I felt in my heart. As I began my daily prayer routine, the Holy Spirit spoke to me and said, "Just speak from your heart." Feeling shocked from hearing the presence of His voice, I paused in disbelief as His voice repeated itself; "Just speak from your heart," the Holy Spirit said to me once more. Then, the Holy Spirit began questioning my communication and how ineffective those methods were in seeking God through prayer. "Why are you searching for me through the hearts of others when you can pray what's in your heart? The Holy Spirit asked. Then he said, "Do not come to me as a replication of others or as hypocrites so often do, but come as yourself and speak from your heart, and I will teach you My heart." At that moment, all the confusion left me, and I felt so much comfort knowing that I could speak to God from my heart. I began to talk to Him without feeling pressured, and as my conversations grew more consistent, He taught me how to speak to Him through His words, and He often guided me to His words as I was praying and having conversations with Him.

It's so ironic how quickly we turn to men searching for a word from God because we're looking for instant answers or results, not understanding the importance of speaking to God and having patience to wait for His response. Patience helps us to sit still and hear God more. He will undoubtedly give wisdom to those who seek knowledge from Him. As it states in ***James 1:5: "If any of you lacks wisdom, let him ask God who gives generously to all without reproach, and it will be given him."*** It was after I became more patient while consistently seeking God for wisdom that I discovered all I needed was His words. I learned the importance of meditating on God's words daily, praying with an open mind, and allowing the Holy Spirit to guide me to a place of peace. With such stability, I better understood how to speak to God and express my heart. It took away the pressure and stress that I felt so often as I was praying.

I have to admit, It was such a relief to be free of so much confusion in my mind. For me, it felt as if a heavy burden was lifted from my heart because, for so many years, I used to feel so much conviction about prayer. I felt my approach to praying was not correct, but God helped me to understand how to communicate with Him properly. He taught me how to pray what's on my heart and share with Him without all the struggles and doubts that were manufactured in my mind when seeking advice from others about how I should pray. It was through God's instructions that I was able to establish a relationship with Him. And today, He continues to teach me how to effectively communicate with Him in ways that please Him. I learned how to pray with purpose, and I also know how to do it consistently. He began to teach me how to pray His words back to Him, and this has undoubtedly helped me to develop a consistent prayer life, praying with purpose.

It has been a great experience learning how to establish a relationship with God and communicate with Him. Our relationship with God is based on our communications with Him. If you struggle with methods taught by others, this usually indicates that it might not be the correct method for you. He instructed me to talk to Him because God already knows the things in our hearts, even before we speak. I always love hearing my dear friend, Minster Tony Williams, say, "Be real with God, and He will certainly be real with you." Yes, indeed, Minister Tony, you said a mouth full. God is real all the time. Go ahead, merely talk to Him!

DAILY PRAYERS AND INSIGHTFUL ENCOURAGEMENTS WEEK 03

Monday

SCRIPTURE:
2 Peter 3:18
but grow in the grace and knowledge of our Lord and Savior Jesus Christ. To Him be the glory both now and forever. Amen.

1 Timothy 4:15
Meditate on these things; give yourself entirely to them, that your progress may be evident to all.

Heavenly Father, may my confidence always be strong in Christ because I know it holds a tremendous and lasting reward. How tempting it is to rely on my abilities instead of trusting you, Father God, to be my guidance and to offer me wisdom as I face challenges each day. Please help me, Father, to overcome my ways of thinking and to blot away any thoughts that hinder my growth. Help me to keep my mind at peace, to discipline my thinking in ways that keep me productive, but above all things, in ways that help me to guard my hearing and harden my heart towards those who seek to lead us away from truth and righteousness. In Jesus name, I pray, Amen.

Tuesday

Striving For Peace

Sometimes, you have to distance yourself from everything that distracts your peace. Peace is a right given to you; it dictates the outcome of your day and life. You must set boundaries to ensure that you do not allow people to hinder your peace. People can be very selfish at times; they will exhaust you in every way possible to get what they need from you, but it's up to you to limit access to your life, to free yourself from people and systems that exploit everything from you for their gain. Why are you so frustrated? Why do you tolerate those who bring drama to your life? Why are you always uncomfortable? Why overly excerpt yourself when you can say no? To not address such questions means to forfeit your peace. Over the past five months, I made a conscious decision to pull back from anything hindering my peace. I had to realize that I cannot be everything to everybody. It took me a long time to realize that people will love you as much as you can do for them, but when I decided to stop calling, stop showing up, and stop being so easily accessible, peace became so evident in my life. It opened my eyes to realize that I was the most significant hindrance to my lack of peace in trying to be a resource to everyone who needed help. The road to peace always begins with you. Stop for a minute and evaluate yourself, and you will see that people are not invading your peace; IT IS YOU, my dear friends! You are forfeiting your peace; until you realize this, PEACE will never exist in your life.

Wednesday

SCRIPTURE:
2 Timothy 1:7
For God has not given us a spirit of fear, but of power and of love and of a sound mind.

Heavenly Father, I am strong today because I keep Your words close in my heart. I am focused today because I keep my mind focused on those things that are above. My strength is in You, Father God. You are my rock, shield, and guidance through a world that has gotten out of control. I do not live in fear, and nor do I live without discipline. 2 **Timothy 1:7** says, **"For God has not given us a spirit of fear, but of power and of love and of a sound mind"** Therefore, it is my prayer, Father God, that I continue to live out of the obedience of your words so that my life is always disciplined and pleasing to You. In Jesus' name, I pray Amen

"Just because you can't hear God speaking back to you, it doesn't mean He's not listening to you"
#PrayerDrivenLife

Thursday

Fear

No matter what goes on around us, fear should never be a part of our mindset. We must always be prepared mentally to defeat the spirit of fear in our minds. Yes, I know we are living in difficult times. Yes, sickness has stricken many. Some people barely make ends meet, but God understands everything you're facing. But you must also understand that FAITH moves God, not fear. It doesn't matter what it looks like; what truly matters is your faith in the midst of what you see. Instead of seeing sickness, I see healing coming forth. Instead of seeing financial situations, I see blessings in my life. Instead of seeing doubts, I see assurances. Having a mindset of faith must be something we practice daily. You can't panic your way out of situations, and *fear is a reaction that produces no results*, but FAITH pleases God! Now is the time, more than ever, to move beyond spiritual immaturity and experience a sense of confidence in our faith. Since Christ has gone ahead of us to secure our salvation, we should have absolute confidence, as a sure and steadfast anchor of our soul, that God will supply our needs and that His grace and mercy are upon us.

SCRIPTURE:
2 Timothy 1:7
For God has not given us a spirit of fear, but of power and of love and of a sound mind.

Friday

SCRIPTURE:
Romans 15:13
Now may the God of hope fill you with all joy and peace in believing, that you may abound in hope by the power of the Holy Spirit.

Romans 5:1
Therefore, having been justified by faith, we have peace with God through our Lord Jesus Christ,

Heavenly Father, my connection to You makes me relevant in life, so my purpose is never to align myself with anything or anyone that's not aligned with You. Help me, Father, to walk each day with Your wisdom upon me so that I approach every encounter with the knowledge of Your words as my guidance to make the best possible decisions for my life. Thank You for never giving up on me, Father God, for always answering my prayers, and for keeping me at a place of peace, especially in a world that struggles with peace daily. I pray for everyone who reads this prayer that you shall sustain them, restore their minds, refocus their purpose, and bring peace to their hearts, just as it says in **Romans 15:13: "Now may the God of hope fill you with all joy and peace in believing, that you may abound in hope by the power of the Holy Spirit."** And **Romans 5:1 says, :Therefore, having been justified by faith, we have peace with God through our Lord Jesus Christ,"** In Jesus name, I pray, Amen.

Saturday

Elevate Your Thinking

It's important never to allow people to become a distraction in your life. At some point in your life, you must ELEVATE YOUR THINKING to a level that takes your mind off people and focus more on God. Do you not know or understand how powerful you are? Do you not know how to tap into your potential? What are your goals in life? What dreams do you have? You see, there is so much in you alone which can drive your focus. There are so many things that you can do to better yourself. Stop wasting your energy and time worrying about what people might think or say about you, and perfect yourself more. Every day, you must TARGET YOUR FOCUS, search deep within yourself, and find something that drives and motivates you. There is an economy that lives in each of us. There are ideas and capabilities just waiting for you to tap into. Don't allow your potential to be dormant while being distracted by anyone or anything unimportant.

SCRIPTURE:
Romans 8:5
For those who live according to the flesh set their minds on the things of the flesh, but those who live according to the Spirit, the things of the Spirit.

Sunday

SCRIPTURE:
Philippians 4:7
and the peace of God, which surpasses all understanding, will guard your hearts and minds through Christ Jesus.

Father God, I pray that peace be upon this nation and that Your words shall restore truth in the hearts of many as we face these spirits leading many to follow false realities. There is no greater time than now that we seek You, Father God, to know Your words and keep them in our hearts daily. I pray for a mind that's always on You, Father. I pray for strength in every area of my life, with hopes that I become more disciplined so that I do not become a slave desiring the things of this world, but instead, I keep my mind focused on those things that are above. Your word says in *Isaiah* **26:3, "You will keep him in perfect peace, Whose mind is stayed on You, Because he trusts in You."** And *Philippians* **4:7 says, "And the peace of God, which surpasses all understanding, will guard your hearts and minds in Christ Jesus."** In Jesus name, I pray Amen.

"Do you trust God, or do you trust that person that's willing to listen?"
#PrayerDrivenLife

Chapter 04
The Challenges Of Self Discipline

PRAYER:

Heavenly Father, I need discipline every day, and I depend on Your words to guide me and lead me in the right direction. Father God, I pray for wisdom and understanding. I pray for a mind always on You and to be equipped through Your words as I journey through life each day. In Jesus' name, I pray. Amen.

SCRIPTURE REFERENCE
HEBREWS 12:11
For the moment all discipline seems painful rather than pleasant, but later it yields the peaceful fruit of righteousness to those who have been trained by it.

SELF DISCIPLINE:

By the time I reached the age of 21, I didn't think much about discipline. My approach to life was to live in ways that pleased me, caring less about discipline. For me, it was more about having the freedom to do whatever I wanted with my life without anyone else's approval. As I became stable enough to move out independently, discipline was missing from my life. I spent countless amounts of time facing the consequences of my choices, influenced mainly by bad habits. Indeed, this is something that hindered my ability to stay focused. At some point, I knew I needed to become more disciplined and desperately needed to add structure to my life.

It takes a lot of patience to develop a disciplined lifestyle, and patience was something that I didn't have when I was young. As I learned to practice patience more, it helped me to sit still and wait on God. It positioned me to hear His voice above everything happening in my life. It helped me become less distracted because I was willing to listen to God more. Of course, waiting on God is not always easy because God's timing doesn't adhere to man's timing, and indeed, He understands what we need better than we do.

When I look back on my life, I realize how much I contributed to most of my failures, and it was because I lacked discipline and there was no structure to how I lived my life. When I was younger, just like with most teens, I became rebellious, and I wasn't interested in living a structured lifestyle, nor did I have any interest in seeking God's word for guidance. But as I grew older and life's challenges began to overwhelm me, there was a greater need for advice, and I knew I had to discipline and structure my life to succeed. God's word helps us structure our lives in ways that keep us from defeating ourselves, but you must commit and submit to His word for it to be effective. How can we obtain discipline without knowing God's word? Knowledge often starts with a commitment to submit your hearing to His word, praying, and meditating daily. Finding a good church home that teaches sound doctrine is significant for spiritual growth. I know many people are quick to say that they don't need to go to church or they don't need a pastor, but in ***Romans 10:14- 21, KJV***, the Bible says otherwise, which says: ***"How then shall they call on him in whom they have not believed? And how shall they believe in him of whom they have not heard? And how shall they hear without a preacher?*** You see, God understands the nature of who we are and knows that many of us are not disciplined enough to teach ourselves, so if God ordained preachers to teach us the word, how can one say he doesn't need teaching? Are you indeed that discipline? Most people who shy away from discipline are usually too prideful to admit to it, but being prideful will destroy you because a prideful person adheres to little discipline. Life without discipline is not a great rule to live your life by.

Now that I've grown much older and wiser, I have no problem gravitating towards discipline. Being in my twenties, I wasn't concerned about tapping into my capabilities or discovering my life's purpose because much of that requires obedience to God's instructions. Yes, my parents taught me to be obedient, and because of that, I stayed out of trouble, but once I gravitated towards making my own decisions, I failed so often.

Life has been a learning curve, and I appreciated the kind of discipline I got from my parents because it put enough fear in me to keep me out of trouble. There's many benefits to learning to live a disciplined lifestyle using God's principles. It gives us a foundation to structure life in ways that build success.

It's never too late, nor are you too old to discipline and structure your life. You must be willing to establish a consistent relationship with God. It would help if you were submissive to his principles and open to corrections, which don't always feel comfortable. Discipline requires lifelong learning while applying God's principles to everyday living. We must constantly feed our minds daily to fight against the warfare that seeks to challenge our existence. Discipline helps us stay on course; it allows us to build a solid foundation that gives us the structure we need in our lives for years to come. Prayer offers us a foundation for communicating with God, it gives us hope, and it also provides us with a foundation which will keep us grounded. Through prayer, He strengthens, guides, and disciplines our minds to get the most out of life. Prayer is our gateway communication to God's heart.

He hears us and loves us unconditionally. It doesn't matter what we face in life; we must never cease praying. We must always trust God, no matter how difficult it might seem. When you become disciplined, it structures you in ways that sustain you. It prepares you for those moments when you have nowhere else to turn but to stand on God's word. **Hebrews 11:12** *said it best: Yes, discipline is painful, but it yields the peaceful fruit of righteousness.*

In times of uncertainties you have to adjust your hearing in order to protect your heart from fear. Too much information can drive your mind in many directions. Guard your hearing!
#PrayerDrivenLife

DAILY PRAYERS
AND INSIGHTFUL ENCOURAGEMENTS
WEEK 04

Monday

SCRIPTURE:
Matthews 5:6
Blessed are those who hunger and thirst for righteousness, For they shall be filled.

Heavenly Father, You have brought peace throughout my surroundings. You keep me in perfect peace because I keep my mind on you. Thank You for separating me from my distractors and for keeping me at a level of focus which helps me to stay productive each day. I pray against all evil assignments against my life. I believe I can do all things through Christ, which strengthens me; therefore, I see the impossible as always possible, and I can accomplish anything I set out to do in this life. Help me to grow stronger in You, to keep this hunger for your words in my heart. Help me always to stay humble and to love even at times when I feel betrayed by others. Keep me at a place, Father God, where I can grow, where Your wisdom and guidance are always upon my life. I desire to succeed in life, but not at the expense of losing my relationship with You, Father God. For it is You who gives me life, and forever I labor to be with You everlasting. In Jesus name, I pray Amen.

Tuesday

The Benefits Of Positive Energy

The most focused-minded people have positive conversations because they understand that positive energy drives purpose. You can become vulnerable to negativity when you don't have a purpose. Not only do you lose focus, but you are also easily influenced or distracted from ever achieving anything meaningful in life. This is why it's essential to guard your heart and hearing, because negativity seeks to plant its seeds in them. As you awaken each day, speak life into your existence. Empower your surroundings with positive confessions, casting out the influence of darkness that seeks you out daily. Stay focused, stay positive, and most of all, keep praying.

SCRIPTURE:
Philippians 4:4-7
Rejoice in the Lord always. Again I will say, rejoice! Let your gentleness be known to all men. The Lord is at hand. Be anxious for nothing, but in everything by prayer and supplication, with thanksgiving, let your requests be made known to God; and the peace of God, which surpasses all understanding, will guard your hearts and minds through Christ Jesus.

Wednesday

SCRIPTURE:
Matthew 5:4
Blessed are those who mourn, for they shall be comforted.

Psalm 34:18
The Lord is near to the brokenhearted and saves the crushed in spirit."
I pray Father God, that healing comes quickly to those who are
mourning and that they shall find comfort and peace in You

The most challenging thing we face in life is losing a loved one. The thought of never seeing that person again, the idea of feeling that the times you spent with them were just not enough. How often do we take life for granted? How often do we take our loved ones for granted? Neither the day nor hour is promised to us; we must use our time on this earth wisely, and our presence to the ones we love must be felt as often as possible because life here was never meant to be forever. Let us join together in praying this prayer . . .

Heavenly Father, I pray for those who are experiencing the loss of a loved one. I pray for those who are struggling to find healing and peace through such a devastating loss. **Matthew 5:4** says, **"Blessed are those who mourn, For they shall be comforted. Psalm 34:18** says, **"The Lord is near to the brokenhearted and saves the crushed in spirit."** I pray Father God, that healing comes quickly to those who are mourning and that they shall find comfort and peace in You, Father God. In Jesus name, I pray Amen.

Many times our emotions both pleasant or unpleasant is usually the results of our thoughts. What are you allowing your mind to get you in today? "
#PrayerDrivenLife

Thursday

Heavenly Father, Your grace is upon us, Your mercies endure forever, You are a merciful God who loves unconditionally. You sent Your words and healed the land to shelter Your people from chaos. Thank You, Father God, for helping us to stay calm in the midst of adversity and to rest in You where peace resides. Father God, today and every day, I put my trust in You, and my thoughts are free from the uncertainties of this world because my mind has stayed on You. Thank You, Father, for the Beauty of the sun, which brightens the sky, for the rain which pours upon us to support life on this earth. It's the simplest things I'm most grateful for, to know that You are God Almighty, who creates all. Many are now stricken with sickness, and I pray for healing to come forth in their bodies, by His stripes, we are healed. I rebuke the spirit of fear that has taken over the minds of many, and I pray that every weapon formed against our health shall be defeated. Your word says in *Psalm* **41:3,** **"The Lord sustains him on his sickbed; in his illness you restore him to full health."** *James* **5:14-16** says, **"The prayer of faith will save the one who is sick, and the Lord will raise him up."** It also says that **"The prayer of a righteous person has great power as it is working,"** Therefore, I release the power of prayer in the atmosphere today and speak healing to all who receive this prayer. I stand in agreement today, Father God, with all the Elders, ministers, and prayer warriors, as You release them throughout all the earth to pray over this land, and no harm shall come against them and their families. In Jesus name, I pray, Amen.

Friday

SCRIPTURE:
1 John 4:7-8
He who does not love does not know God, for God is love. Beloved, let us love one another, for love is of God; and everyone who loves is born of God and knows God. He who does not love does not know God, for God is love

Heavenly Father, LOVE is who You are. LOVE is who I desire to be, for You have shown love to us since the creation of humankind. Help us, Father God, to get back to the basics of living where love is at the forefront in all of us. Restore us to having compassion for others, to be more patient with one another with true love in our hearts. Your words in *1 John 4:8:* **"Anyone who does not love does not know You, Father God, because You are LOVE.** We need so much more of You, Father God, as we need to lay down our selfishness and become like Jesus, who sacrificed so much that we might live forever with You. Forgive us Father, restore our hearts and remove the influence of this world from within us. Bring us back to a place where love conquers any despicable behaviors that try to rise within us. In Jesus' name, I pray for *Patience, Peace, Restoration, Tolerance,* and, most importantly, to restore *LOVE* in the hearts of every man, woman, and child. Amen!

Saturday

With God, Anything Is Possible

You can be amazed at what you can accomplish if you put forth the effort to do it. I strongly believe in **Philippians 4:13,** which says, *"I can do all things through Christ who strengthens me."* Every day, we should challenge ourselves to do better and be better. Doubt should never be a part of your thought process; even if it looks complicated, your greatest strength should always be your faith. Who amongst you believe in yourself? Do you know who you are or to whom you belong? Those who genuinely know our God understand the power that lives in us. Therefore, you will not only be amazed at what you can accomplish, but you will approach life with the most significant amount of confidence, knowing that all things are possible to those who believe.

Sunday

SCRIPTURE:
Psalms 34:18
That the Lord is near to the brokenhearted and saves the crushed in spirit.

Heavenly Father, help us to find strength each day in your word, even through the most difficult challenges we face each day. Comfort the weak that they may find strength in You, Lord, and give peace to those who need peace more than ever. Every day is a new day to be grateful for life and to be thankful for the memories that we once shared with loved ones who are no longer with us. Today, I awaken with a spirit of appreciation, knowing that You are God almighty, who's grace is upon my life. I worship you, Father God, when times are great, as well as through the storms, because even in my darkest days, **Psalms 34:18** reminds me, **"That the Lord is near to the brokenhearted and saves the crushed in spirit."** Your steadfast love endures forever, Father God, and this is the assurance we have to know that no matter how much we endure throughout this life, we never endure it alone because Your presence is always upon us. In Jesus name I pray, amen.

"Keeping your mind filled with self limiting thoughts, can hinder your growth"

#PrayerDrivenLife

Chapter 05
Struggling To Forgive

SCRIPTURE REFERENCE
MATTHEW 6:14-15
For if you forgive others their trespasses, your heavenly Father will also forgive you, but if you do not forgive others their trespasses, neither will your Father forgive your trespasses.

PRAYER:
Heavenly Father, help me always to keep forgiveness in my heart never to allow bitterness to live within me. It is my prayer that I am always quick to forgive and slow to anger, always prepared to allow LOVE to dictate my responses so that I am always in Your will, Father God, and always in Your peace. In Jesus' name, I pray, Amen

STRUGGLING TO FORGIVE

One of the most difficult challenges I ever faced was learning how to deal with forgiveness. Years ago, I spent so much of my life harboring bitterness toward my Father because of his lack of presence in my life. It's not that he wasn't a great person or even a great father because he was a great provider for my siblings who lived under his roof. But for me, I felt neglected and cheated out of life. I had never experienced what it was like to have a father's presence in my life. My grandmother raised me, and my mother supported me, and I am grateful for their sacrifices. I will always be thankful for my upbringing, but I couldn't help but think how I could have been much more disciplined by having a male figure to look up to.

As a child growing up, even though I had this bitterness towards My father, I still loved and respected him deep down inside. It's not that he wasn't a good person; instead, he was just a man who put himself in many bad situations by having many kids he couldn't support. His lack of presence in my life didn't do as much harm as it could have because I was under the best of care, raised by my grandmother. The most important thing I learned in my adolescent years is how bitterness could affect one's life and hinder a person's growth. I also learned how bitterness can affect a person's ability to forgive. I failed to understand that harboring resentment in your heart can cause you to develop hate, hindering your growth and peace.

At some point in my life, I allowed bitterness toward my father to poison my mind so much that I didn't care. I often tried to deal with the emotions of not having my father around by attempting to make him nonexistent in my mind. I would always find ways to live my life the best I could without ever allowing any thoughts of him to exist in my mind. After a while of suppressing those emotions and feelings towards my father, it gave me a false sense of healing. With such a false sense of healing, I could no longer feel anger or bitterness toward my father because I suppressed those feelings deep within my heart. I didn't think about him and tried to convince myself that he never existed. But certainly, I was fooling myself, being naive about how I was feeling. I fooled myself into thinking I was no longer harboring feelings of bitterness, and indeed, I was wrong. I suppressed those feelings instead of dealing with them head-on.

As I matured and my relationship with God became more consistent, God helped me deal with many of the challenges I often faced. I prayed constantly, trusting and believing that God would heal my heart and deliver me from my destructive thoughts, which wasn't healthy for my mindset.

I was blind, not willing to admit how much I was mentally being affected, and I had no idea how to deal with it.

As I was praying one morning, the Holy Spirit said, "You often pray about how difficult life is, but life is not your problem. He said, "Your biggest problems are the things you have hidden in your heart." And I asked with curiosity, "What are the things I have hidden in my heart, Lord?" And He answered me by saying, "It's Bitterness and Unforgiveness." The Holy Spirit began to tell me that suppressing my emotions towards my father and not addressing them affected me in many ways. He said it would be impossible for me to find peace and forgiveness until I let go of this sin in my heart. I was shocked at first, especially when the Holy Spirit said Unforgiveness Was A Sin". Truly something I didn't know at the time. Still, when I began to examine the words spoken to me, I realized, throughout those years, how much I had lived with bitterness and unforgiveness in my heart and how it was silently affecting how I lived my life and my relationship with others.

After talking to God, I sought Him more for healing and deliverance. As He began to heal my heart and alter my thoughts, I learned to let go of bitterness, and it allowed God to heal me as time passed. I no longer hated my father, and neither did I have any resentment towards him. More and more, I appreciate that I could tell him I loved him while he was alive, and I understand today how God has healed my heart and helped me in ways that have allowed me to forgive him and move beyond unforgiveness. I'm grateful for my deliverance because I could tell him I loved him without bitterness. Through my redemption, I realized how powerful forgiveness is and how important it is to forgive quickly because life is short. Don't allow death to catch you unprepared. A forgiving heart helps to restore relationships, but most of all, it pleases God.

"Failure is an opportunity to grow"
#PrayerDrivenLife

DAILY PRAYERS
AND INSIGHTFUL ENCOURAGEMENTS
WEEK 05

Monday

SCRIPTURE:

James 4:7
Therefore submit to God. Resist the devil and he will flee from you.

Ephesians 6:11
Put on the whole armor of God, that you may be able to stand against the wiles of the devil.

Heavenly Father, every day, I strive to walk with humility and kindness, but that's not always easy when you're often challenged by certain spirits whose primary assignment is to hinder your journey. But I give no place or thought to any enemy assignments against my life because I know that the devil in hell cannot defeat me. After all, you have purposed my life for greater things. Your word says in **James 4:7, "That if I submit to God. Resist the devil and he will flee from you."** And **Ephesians 6:11 says, "Put on the whole armor of God, that you may be able to stand against the wiles of the devil**." These words are my foundation, and It is my strength, my shield to know that if I keep Your words in my heart, Father God, no weapon formed against my life shall prosper, nor shall it bring fear to my heart. In Jesus name, I pray, Amen.

Tuesday

A Greater Focus To Improve Me

I learned long ago that focusing on self-improvement is more important than anything in my life because there is nothing more challenging than ME. So often, we put so much focus on trying to change others, but what about me? What about focusing on changing me? Through all the experiences of our lives, many of us are still living with some of our life experiences, things we thought were behind us but are still affecting our lives daily. The hurt and pain that we have suppressed inside never healed. Behaviors and habits we never truly overcame, but we've ignored them for so long, it gives us the illusion that they no longer exist. I realize I'm a work in progress, and the challenges of who I am needs improvement more often than I care to admit. This is why I'm less critical of others, free from the judgment of others, and more focused on developing a better me. Every day, I pray for stability and peace, and most of all, I pray that God will always keep my eyes open for improvements to myself. In Jesus name, I pray Amen.

SCRIPTURE:
Ephesians 4:15-16
but, speaking the truth in love, may grow up in all things into Him who is the head, Christ from whom the whole body, joined and knit together by what every joint supplies, according to the effective working by which every part does its share, causes growth of the body for the edifying of itself in love.

Wednesday

SCRIPTURE:
Proverbs 16:9
A man's heart plans his way, But the Lord directs his steps.

Psalm 32:8
will instruct you and teach you in the way you should go; I will guide you with My eye.

Thank You, Father God, in advance for ordering my steps today. Thank You, Father, for conditioning my heart with love and patience as I journey throughout this day. The beauty of each day is knowing that You are continuously guiding my life. There are no limits to my success because of You. Father, I pray for Your peace all around me, and I live with the confidence that Your grace is sufficient for all my needs. Your presence is mighty, sustaining me throughout each day. I depend on You Father, and my heart is always open to Your corrections. Today, I speak life, and I speak healing throughout my body, mind and as well as in the lives of everyone who reads this prayer. I speak peace throughout my surroundings, and I cast away every demonic assignment that seeks to hinder my progress today. In Jesus name, I pray For us all. Amen. ***Proverbs 16:9, Psalm 32:8***

Thursday

Striving To Empower My Thinking

I spend a lot of time ignoring myself; sometimes, I don't want to hear anything I have to say unless I'm encouraging myself unless I'm empowering myself, or speaking powerful words to myself. I refuse to allow my mind to go unregulated, to think without a purpose. I have no problem telling me to shut up! Be quiet, I say! If I don't have anything positive to say, then I silence myself until my mind is under the submission of positive thinking. I understand that everything concerning me starts with my mind, how I mentally think, and how I process things mentally. Therefore, my day begins with nurturing my mind and empowering my thinking while using God's word for guidance and wisdom. Yes, sometimes I fail throughout this process, but I don't give up because I know that this life's journey is a RACE I'm destined to win!

Friday

SCRIPTURE:
Proverbs 16:9
A man's heart plans his way, But the Lord directs his steps.

Psalm 32:8
will instruct you and teach you in the way you should go; I will guide you with My eye.

It doesn't matter how positive you set out to be each day, there will always be negativity trying to cling onto you. This is why it's so important to be positive, as well as to stay encouraged and be driven with your goals and your life's purpose. Every day, you must have a plan and be prepared to execute it. You must set your mind on that which is above and not on the things of this world. Yes, there will be challenges. Yes, there will be distractions, but a focused mind filled with purpose has already been equipped to overcome such things. Let's pray this prayer together . . . .

Heavenly Father, help me to stay driven and purpose minded, to manage my time each day so that I can effectively achieve my goals throughout this day. Thank You, Father, in advance for your patience in letting your plans manifest in my life. Help me to be a resource and not a dependent. To glorify You through my behavior, my character, and my integrity, with hopes that others might see Your presence in my life, guiding me and ordering my steps daily. In Jesus name I pray, Amen. **Psalm 37:23, Psalm 32:8.**

Saturday

Self Appreciation

Often, when you lose perspective of how beautiful of a person you are, you seek ways to validate the beauty of who you are, so much to the point it clouds your identity. It would help if you learned to appreciate yourself and put your energy towards being your best. Being excellent starts with a mindset of believing that you are truly unique. There's a natural beauty in each of us, and when you learn to tap into the beauty of who you are, you develop respect for yourself and always carry yourself with decency and high standards. Don't allow the norms to convince you that defining your beauty means you have to expose yourself to lusting eyes or disgrace your body in disrespectful ways. Being excellent is as simple as knowing who you are and whom you belong to while allowing Christ to shine through you.

SCRIPTURE:
Matthew 5:16
Let your light so shine before men, that they may see your good works and glorify your Father in heaven.

Sunday

SCRIPTURE:
Romans 12:1-2
I beseech you therefore, brethren, by the mercies of God, that you present your bodies a living sacrifice, holy, acceptable to God, *which is* your reasonable service. And do not be conformed to this world, but be transformed by the renewing of your mind, that you may prove what *is* that good and acceptable and perfect will of God.

Heavenly Father, as a believer, I can be assured that a glorious kingdom awaits me, a far greater place than I can ever imagine. I cannot allow myself to be hindered by the events of this world, for this world is destined to destroy itself. I must encourage myself each day, because of Your mercy, to offer my body as a living sacrifice, doing that which is holy and pleasing unto You Father. For this is my true and proper worship, Father, I understand how important it is not to pattern myself after this world but to be transformed by the renewing of my mind to serve your perfect will for my life. Oh Father God, I need Your presence in my life each day, everyday becomes a struggle to arrest my flesh from the temptations of this world, but I understand who I am in Christ Jesus, a chosen disciple to teach the gospel of Jesus Christ. And this is my confidence as a believer that you will not let me fail this assignment. In Jesus name I pray Amen. ***Romans 12:1-2, Matthew 16:24, 2 Corinthians 6:14.***

"PURPOSE minded people don't mind your criticism? It's because their level of FOCUS is above your comprehension, which makes your criticism irrelevant"

#PrayerDrivenLife

EIGHT WISDOM QUOTES FOR MOTIVATION & SELF-IMPROVEMENT

Never expect life to be easy, but always have the highest expectations of your abilities to conquer life and accomplish the things you desire in life. Often, you will face challenges throughout your journey, but you can easily overcome such difficulties with FAITH, CONSISTENCY, and HARD WORK. You must understand that success doesn't come without hard work.
Matthew's 21:22
Galatians 6:9

Be less critical of others and focus on correcting and critiquing yourself. Discipline is essential and should be your ultimate goal. The worst thing you can do in life is to think too highly of yourself, so much to the point you feel that corrections and discipline are not necessary. Trust me . . . It's absolutely necessary!
Matthew 7:1-5
Hebrews 12:11

When you align your life using the principles of God's words, He will guide you. James 1:5 Says, "If any of you lacks wisdom, let him ask God, who gives generously to all without reproach, and it will be given him." Life is not that complicated. We only make it difficult when we fail to structure it properly. God's principles offer us the best foundation to structure our lives.
Romans 12:2

Challenge yourself daily to be great, and always remember that consistency can quickly turn your limitations into possibilities. Faith, as well as your confessions, can often play a significant part in elevating a successful, fulfilling life.
Philippians 4:13
Matthew 19:26

Learning how to channel your focus towards positive things is a great way to become less distracted by the negativity surrounding you. You must learn to defeat distractions, and what better way to beat your distractions than with a FOCUS mind? A focused mind is a productive mind.
Colossians 3:2

Surround yourself with positive friends who encourage you motivate you, and with people who appreciate and value your friendship above all things. Friendship should never be overly taxing, neither should it be without boundaries.
Proverbs 18:24
John 15:13
Proverbs 17:17

Nothing changes in life until you decide you've had enough. It's essential to take control of your life and not allow the things surrounding you to dictate the outcome. Learn to use the power of God's word to command things to work in your favor. You have the

power to Speak It, Command It, and Expect It. Just know in your heart with confidence that your confessions are power!
Ephesians 1:11

Strive to always treat people with kindness and respect. Jesus commanded us to Love; therefore, love and compassion are excellent characteristics. When we allow LOVE to be the example that defines us, not only does it define our character, but it also pleases God.
Galatians 5:22-23

DAILY PRAYERS
AND INSIGHTFUL ENCOURAGEMENTS
WEEK 06

Monday

SCRIPTURE:
Romans 12:1-2
I beseech you therefore, brethren, by the mercies of God, that you present your bodies a living sacrifice, holy, acceptable to God, which is your reasonable service. And do not be conformed to this world, but be transformed by the renewing of your mind, that you may prove what is that good and acceptable and perfect will of God.

Heavenly Father, thank You for establishing in me a desire and hunger for truth and wisdom, for I know that we live in the last days where truth can be easily distorted and devalued by those who claim to represent You. I pray for those who are lost and those who are misguided. I pray against this evil that has brought so much ungodliness to our society. I know the enemy comes to steal, kill, and destroy, but You did not give us the spirit of fear; therefore, I reject this evil upon us. I pray for Your protection, Father, against the influences of this world as You continue to guide my heart, mind, and speech. For on this day, Father, I make the decision of faith to surrender wholly under your authority and choose to walk in the light, in alignment with Christ, my Lord and Savior. In Jesus name, I pray Amen.
Philippians 2:12-13; and 1 John 1:7-9

Tuesday

Above All Things, Trust God

Everything in our life happens for a reason, and when you can't understand it, it's not wise to continue to wrestle with your faith because doubts will have you looking for answers outside of God's word. His words are truth, and it surpasses all our understanding. Trusting God empowers our faith because we learn to be patient and trust Him. God's word shall prevail over our lives. It should be above every decision we make, despite what we're going through and regardless of our feelings and opinions. Let us pray . . .

Heavenly Father, my most tremendous success is when I genuinely understand You. Above all things, it is Your will, Father, and never my will, and I pray with patience so that I do not hinder Your purpose for my life. In Jesus name, I pray, Amen. ***Ephesians 1:11***

SCRIPTURE:
Luke 22:42
saying, "Father, if it is Your will, take this cup away from Me; nevertheless not My will, but Yours, be done."
Jeremiah 29:11
For I know the thoughts that I think toward you, says the Lord, thoughts of peace and not of evil, to give you a future and a hope.

Wednesday

SCRIPTURE:
Romans 12:1-2
I beseech you therefore, brethren, by the mercies of God, that you present your bodies a living sacrifice, holy, acceptable to God, which is your reasonable service. And do not be conformed to this world, but be transformed by the renewing of your mind, that you may prove what is that good and acceptable and perfect will of God.

Colossians 3:2
Set your mind on things above, not on things on the earth. For you died, and your life is hidden with Christ in God. When Christ *who is* our life appears, then you also will appear with Him in glory.

Father God, your grace upon my life each day keeps me in peace. I know that I cannot lose focus, but I must keep my eyes on the things above and not the foolishness of this world. Father, I pray for wisdom, to know Your truth, and to reject those leading Your people astray. Save me, Father, not only from the wickedness of this nation but also from myself. Examine me each day, and help me to see myself in the mirror so that I can correct those things about me that are not pleasing to You. Father, I rejoice in Your glory; I wait patiently, knowing that Your presence is near, even in the mists of chaos. I desire to serve You, to know Your purpose for my life, and to live each day fulfilling this purpose before my time has expired on this earth. In Jesus name, I pray, Amen. ***James 1:5,***

- ENCOURAGING INSIGHTS -

DECEITFUL SPIRITS:

The days have come when a deceitful spirit shall deceive the world into believing that which is evil was sent from God. It is essential more than ever to strengthen your relationship with Jesus, for there are many worldly leaders who falsely claim to be the savior sent by God to lead His people. Beware of false prophets, misguided leaders who claim to hear from God, those who try to cancel out Jesus, who is the true savior of God's people, and His character exemplifies the righteousness of God, which no man upon this earth can be compared to Him. Beware of those who say that God sent this one or that one to lead a nation. Still, their character and behavior are far from anything Christ-like, for this is the works of the enemy who comes to steal, kill, destroy, and confuse the mind of those who have become dependent upon men for truth without laboring and studying to know what is truth as it is written. I pray for the innocent minds of this nation; I pray against the wicked influences that continue to bring confusion to the world. For there is a spirit of deception upon our country; its purpose is to deceive a nation of people who have opened their hearts to evil. A nation of people who have become comfortable with even those things which God hates and that which is an abomination unto Him. Have mercy on us, Father, forgive us, for we have shamed the righteousness of Your words without rebuke. Save us from ourselves as we continue on this blind path of destruction!

Thursday

SCRIPTURE:
Psalm 51:12
Restore to me the joy of Your salvation, And uphold me by Your generous Spirit.

Heavenly Father, as each day passes, I am grateful for all of life's experiences and all the things You have brought me through. Thank You for restoring my mind each day, for giving me the wisdom to separate my thoughts from the troubles of this world by keeping my mind on the things above. Every day, my desire to serve You grows stronger. My hunger for righteousness keeps me from the deceptions of this world so that I am not led astray by false teachings. Thank You, Father, for being my strength, shield, and protector each day; your presence is forever strong in my life. In Jesus name, I pray, Amen.

Friday

SCRIPTURE:
Jeremiah 29:11
For I know the thoughts that I think toward you, says the Lord, thoughts of peace and not of evil, to give you a future and a hope.

Proverbs 19:21
There are many plans in a man's heart, Nevertheless the Lord's counsel that will stand.

Every day I am grateful for life, I have to know where God is leading me, and be positioned to hear His voice and seek His wisdom daily. For His words teach us many things about life, therefore, life should never be a guessing game, but I must have a plan. There must be discipline and structure in my life because it's not wise for me to live life as if it is an experiment, but I must live it with purpose. Join me with this prayer . . .

Heavenly Father, help me to fulfill Your purpose for my life and to discipline my hearing so that I am not led astray through my understanding but always guided through Your wisdom as I learn to hear Your voice. Forgive me for wanting to do things my way, and thank You for Your guidance and instructions, which keep me on the right path. My life is unstable without structure, Father, and I understand there is no joy in life without fulfilling Your purpose because fulfilling Your purpose will be my ultimate life achievement. In Jesus name I pray, Amen ***Ephesians 2:10.***

Saturday

Relationship With God

The time to know God is every day of our lives, staying connected to Him, seeking Him, and developing a relationship with Him. When you create a relationship with God, you don't treat Him like an emergency room, but no matter what happens or what goes on, you stand on His words because His words bring peace in every situation. It is faith that moves God. He understands everything we go through, and He wants us to trust Him and know His heart because He loves us and will never leave us alone. Often, just crying out to God becomes ineffective, not because we think that He doesn't hear us, but because we don't honestly know Him enough to know that He hears our cries. To know God is to have PEACE. To know Him is to have FAITH. To know God is to understand His Grace upon your life. Therefore, you understand that no matter how difficult things might seem, how impossible they might appear at this moment, I Trust You, Lord, With Every Area Of My Life. Therefore, I silence myself and rejoice and pray through it all.

Sunday

SCRIPTURE:
1 John 4:7-9
Beloved, let us love one another, for love is of God; and everyone who loves is born of God and knows God. He who does not love does not know God, for God is love. In this the love of God was manifested toward us, that God has sent His only begotten Son into the world, that we might live through Him.

LOVE had to be very important because it was something that Jesus commanded of us all before He died. Jesus love every one of us, even those who crucified Him. He is our greatest example of what true love is and should be. Love is more powerful than any influence upon this earth. Love is a cost-free emotion that requires very little energy. When it's pure and sincere from the heart, its ability to neutralize every negative influence cancels out those who seek to alter one's spirits with fear, hate, and divisiveness . . . Pray this prayer with me

Lord Jesus, thank You for Your LOVE AND SACRIFICES, for loving us so much that You would die for us. Have mercy on this nation who have denied others out of fear, hate, and influence. Position the hearts of the people of this nation to reject hatred and be filled with LOVE and compassion towards your people. Lord, your words say in 1 ***John 4:8, "He who does not love does not know God, for God is love."*** LOVE is our greatest identity, which genuinely separates us from the world because You are LOVE; that is the characteristic I strive to possess daily! Amen!

"The identity of who you are is a lot more than the person you see in the mirror, when you truly understand who you are, and whom you belong to, life will be much easier to conquer"

#PrayerDrivenLife

Chapter 06
What Is Your Ministry?

SCRIPTURE REFERENCE

2 Peter 1:10

Therefore, brethren, be even more diligent to make your call and election sure, for if you do these things you will never stumble;

PRAYER:

Heavenly Father, thank You for this call upon my life to do great things to promote Your Kingdom and to spread the gospel for all to hear. Help me to stay humble along this journey and always show love and compassion towards others, even as there are obstacles along my path. Father God, I trust You at all times. Your grace is sufficient, and Your mercies endure everlasting; therefore, I can do all things through Christ, which strengthens me daily. Father God, in Jesus' name, I pray for wisdom and understanding. I pray for Your guidance to always be with me as I strive to serve as Your humble servant daily. In Jesus name, I pray, Amen.

WHAT IS YOUR MINISTRY?:

I've learned throughout the years the importance of developing a relationship with God because if you don't know or understand God's calling for your life, people will use you and steer you into directions far from the calling God has placed on your life. It's important to know who you are and whom you belong to. Don't just get caught up in the routines of ministry, but understand your calling above all things and connect yourself to a church that's more interested in helping you develop and prepare for the calling God has placed on your life.

You can quickly become frustrated with the Church when It becomes more about serving leaders and less about serving God's purpose. When people see your capabilities or gifts, they quickly align that to be your ministry and gradually try to convince you to accept it as your leadership responsibility.

But having the capabilities to do multiple things, does not mean this is your calling. Your ministry is often greater than what many can see. The abovementioned reason is why your relationship with God becomes crucial so that you understand the purpose and call upon your life.

Some of the most powerful ministries are likely stalled right amid the Church, often filled with people who either do not understand their purpose or people who genuinely do not understand the potential God has placed in them. What is your passion? What is it that you're most gifted in doing? How can you use it for discipleship, to impact lives, and to save souls? Questions such as these are often the starting point of discovering your purpose or discovering what your ministry might be. When I began to meditate, pray, and talk to God daily, I began to understand my potential and how it benefits the Church. God helped me to understand that my gifts wasn't just to serve the Church, but it was for a greater purpose to enhance God's kingdom and and also to improve my financial stability. The Bible says that your gift will make room for you, but if you position yourself with selfish-minded people, your gifts will enslave you and serve no one but those who seek to exploit it.

Many of us waste so much of our time dormant in the Church. The moment God calls us to ministry, we quickly lose sight of the preparation needed to fulfill our purpose of becoming effective disciples of God's kingdom. Yes, It's so easy to get caught up in the glamor of the position, clearly not understanding that Church is just the starting point for our journey ahead. We are first one body in Christ, which is just one piece of the puzzle to fulfill His commandments to teach the gospel of Jesus Christ and glorify God throughout the land. Sadly enough, many of us get stalled in the routines of the Church, not understanding God's Purpose for our lives. Jesus called us to discipleship first and foremost. He didn't call us to get caught up in the

Church's process and routine; we are called to discipleship, to prepare ourselves, and to learn to go out into the world, reaching lost souls and expanding God's kingdom.

Now, let's go back to that thing that's driving you the most, that passion inside you, driving every part of your heart and mind. That gift that brings out the best of who you are. That's your ministry! That's who you are! That's what you're anointed and called to do! The key to figuring it all out begins with our connection to the body of Christ, but most importantly, through our relationship with God. God has gifted in You for a reason. You are purposed to be you, anointed to fulfill the promises of God in you.

To discover and develop your ministry, you must be in a place where you can grow, starting with your relationship with God. When you seek God for wisdom, He will guide you under the covering of a Pastor who will mentor you and help you grow into the person God has anointed you to be. Don't just place yourself under any Pastor. You need a pastor who's after God's heart and teaches sound doctrine in ways you can understand and confirm through God's words.

Many things are lacking with so many leaders in our churches today, and character often sits at the top of the list. A person who shows lousy character or integrity could never be a good steward over God's people, but those who truly have a servant's heart and a compassionate heart for God's people will always stand out. When you develop a strong relationship with God, He will position your heart and guide you throughout your journey in ministry.

We often place ourselves in places and positions because we assume this is where God wants us to be, but is this the place we truly belong? Are you genuinely exercising your gift, or do you position yourself in places or areas where specific talents are needed, often overlooking the true purpose of your calling?

One morning, in my meditation, I recalled that the Holy Spirit proposed a few questions that helped me understand why it's essential to establish a relationship with God to understand the calling God has placed upon my life. Although people mean well, many will never truly take the time to help you grow into your calling. As I was meditating and praying, the Holy Spirit spoke to me and asked me, "Why are you so dormant? Do you know who you are? Do you not understand your purpose?" At that moment, I could not answer the question, nor did I get an answer from the voice that spoke to me. But those questions alone prompted my thinking and aligned my thought process. It made me realize there was more to me than I saw. It helped me understand that although I was skillful, something even greater within me had been dormant, and I wasn't working to bring it out. Yes, It's so true that You can't sit around and wait for others to discover and bring out the purpose of God in you, but instead, you must labor in God's word to indeed find out who you are, to fulfill the calling God has placed upon your life. Even I have lived a significant portion of my life not knowing my true purpose and calling, only to be questioned by the Holy Spirit; "Why are you so dormant?" Because of those questions, God opened my eyes and revealed His truth. Many times, when God calls you, It might not be what you or others want to hear, but all that truly matters is what God decides for your life. Now, I propose this question to you. What is your ministry? What is it that God called you to do? Whatever it is, it's vital that you Labor to find the answers to God's Calling for your life.

DAILY PRAYERS AND INSIGHTFUL ENCOURAGEMENTS WEEK 07

Monday

SCRIPTURE:
1 corinthians 13:4-8
Love suffers long and is kind; love does not envy; love does not parade itself, is not puffed up; does not behave rudely, does not seek its own, is not provoked, thinks no evil; does not rejoice in iniquity, but rejoices in the truth; bears all things, believes all things, hopes all things, endures all things. Love never fails. But whether there are prophecies, they will fail; whether there are tongues, they will cease; whether there is knowledge, it will vanish away.

Heavenly Father, help me to always love each day with a forgiving heart and a spirit without judgment. Every day, I strive to be of good character, showing compassion for those in need and being kind to those who are unkind, with hopes that your glory in me brings about change in others. Father, I pray for my family and my friends. I pray for those who have lost their way. Please help me, Father, find strength within myself in a world that is often demanding and constantly testing my patience. Every day, I need Your guidance; I depend on Your words to empower my thinking and restore my heart to peace. Your words says in **Isaiah 26:3, "You will keep him in perfect peace, whose mind is stayed on You because he trusts in You."** I Trust You, Lord, In Every Area Of My Life. In Jesus name, I pray, Amen.

Tuesday

GETTING THROUGH YOUR SITUATIONS

You never know what people face throughout their lives, but sadly enough, many people might not be mature enough or wise enough to talk to you when you're going through certain situations. This is why It's so essential to develop a relationship with God. Learn to speak to Him first and wait for Him to either give you the wisdom to deal with the situation or to send someone who will give you good advice on how to get through your situation. Life requires a lot of patience, and we often need patience because it helps us to sit still and allow God to help us. Instant solutions are what many of us desire, but the experiences and lessons we learn from them will help us grow. I know that I've made many bad choices and decisions throughout my life, and it is through my mistakes that I have become much wiser. I thank God that He didn't just bail me out but allowed me to work my faith through the process. I'm much better and more robust because I allowed God through His word to rehabilitate me. I was delivered because the grace of God is upon my life, and He watches over me. I learn to be obedient and open to corrections and discipline. I know how to humble myself in ways that the word of God can guide my life to the place I am today. Yes, I'm far from perfect, but I continue to work on improving my life with the hope of finishing this race successfully!!

Wednesday

SCRIPTURE:
Romans 8:26
Likewise the Spirit also helps in our weaknesses. For we do not know what we should pray for as we ought, but the Spirit Himself makes intercession for us with groanings which cannot be uttered.

Isaiah 11:2
The Spirit of the Lord shall rest upon Him, The Spirit of wisdom and understanding, The Spirit of counsel and might, The Spirit of knowledge and of the fear of the Lord.

Our existence is challenged every day because the enemy understands that he must never allow you to succeed at being great. He constantly puts roadblocks before you; he exploits obstacles often created by our behavior or our mindset when we do not align ourselves correctly with God . . .

Heavenly Father, thank You for ordering my steps today and keeping me aligned with Your words. Thank You for the presence of Your Spirit in my life, which guides and instructs me throughout each day. I bind every hindering spirit that seeks to disrupt my assignment today and cast out every thought that isn't designed to prosper my life and bring peace to my thinking. Thank You, Father, for every test I face, every trial, and every situation, whether bad or good. For I believe You have prepared me for this day, to claim victory and to conquer it in every possible way. In Jesus name, I pray. Amen!

"If you are not careful, the way you think can alter your position . . . What are you allowing your mind to get you in today?"
#*PrayerDrivenLife*

Thursday

BEING CRITICAL OF OTHERS

I used to spend a lot of my time being critical of others until one day, I decided to examine my own life, and suddenly, I realized that I was just as jacked up as the people I was being critical of. You know it's often uncomfortable to evaluate yourself, especially when you're comfortable living or being a certain way. Still, you can only experience growth once you face the person you see in the mirror. Many of us are so afraid of change and often find ourselves in denial about certain things in our lives that are hindering our growth. But change is usually necessary as each day we must adjust ourselves and position our minds and hearts against the influences of this world to ensure that we are structured in ways that not only can the world not defeat us, but also we do not defeat ourselves Let's pray this prayer together . . .

Heavenly Father, it is my prayer to always be in Your presence as Your light shines upon my soul, remove anything within me that does not belong, and strengthen me in ways so that I always live my life pleasing You. In Jesus name, I pray. Amen
Romans 12:2, and Romans 8:8

Friday

SCRIPTURE:
Exodus 15:2
The Lord is my strength and song,
And He has become my salvation;
He is my God, and I will praise Him;
My father's God, and I will exalt Him.

Heavenly Father, thank You for empowering me each day and being my strength when things are not at their best. Every day is new, and I am grateful for life and all you have done for me. Father, I pray for those dealing with sickness today; I pray that the weak shall become strong and the lost shall be restored unto Your righteousness. Thank You, Father, in advance for enlarging my territory and positioning the hearts of others to be a blessing in my life. Thank You Father, for helping me keep my heart in a great place and giving me a heart that loves without conditions or judgment. In Jesus name, I pray for peace to be the outcome of this day; amen

Saturday

HOW CAN I IMPROVE ME

I often ask myself questions all the time. How can I improve myself? How can I become more impactful, not only in my life but also in the lives of others? Am I truly making a difference in life? Have I learned to tap into my greatest potential? How can we be so concerned about other people's lives when we often face many challenges and unanswered questions concerning our own lives? Every day, I pray for a hunger for wisdom, to seek knowledge, and to truly understand how to live and improve my life. I have always desired to know God's purpose for my life and strive daily to fulfill His purpose. Life is too short; the journey will not wait for me; therefore, I need to live each day with an urgency. This is why I often pray . . .

Heavenly Father, please don't let me live a moment, an hour, a day, not even a second outside your will. Strengthen me each day to reject sin, to always be open to discipline, and consistently seek guidance and wisdom daily. In Jesus name, I pray.

Sunday

SCRIPTURE:
Psalm 37:23
The steps of a good man are ordered by the Lord,
And He delights in his way.

Psalm 32:8
I will instruct you and teach you in the way you should go; I will guide you with My eye.

Father God, the beauty of each day is knowing that my steps are ordered by You, and my assignment is to be the best I can be. There is no me without You Father God, and I'm grateful that you chose me. My desire is to know Your will, to live according to your righteousness, and never to stray far from you. I need You in my life daily Father, and I depend on You to instruct me, teach me and to help me to grow into a better person that reflects the presence of Your Spirit upon my life. Lord God, I worship You, In Your presence I sing praises to Your Holy name. I give honor to You Father God for being head of my life. Your patience towards me never cease to amaze me, even at times when I've grown far from You, Your patience never left me. Oh how I long the day, when heaven open it's doors for us, so that we could live everlasting with you. In Jesus name I pray, Amen.

"From the moment you open your eyes each morning, there will probably be a few challenges awaiting you. But I encourage you today... You have the POWER to OVERCOME them!!"

#PrayerDrivenLife

Chapter 07
Self Inflicted Wounds

SCRIPTURE REFERENCE
Galatians 5:19-21
Now the works of the flesh are evident, which are: adultery, fornication, uncleanness, lewdness, idolatry, sorcery, hatred, contentions, jealousies, outbursts of wrath, selfish ambitions, dissensions, heresies, envy, murders, drunkenness, revelries, and the like; of which I tell you beforehand, just as I also told you in time past, that those who practice such things will not inherit the kingdom of God.

PRAYER:
Heavenly Father, as each day passes, I pray for discipline, not only for my actions but especially my mindset. Help me to find guidance through Your words, to sustain me, to help me learn to develop patience above all things. Search my heart, Father God, and purify it with love and compassion so that humbleness is not a struggle but it becomes a daily walk. Keep me free from **judgment** *as I repent from my sins, as I acknowledge sin and flee far from it. Father God, my concerns are never perfection but to be perfected by You because You said in* **2 Corinthians** *12:9,* **"My grace is sufficient for you, for My strength is made perfect in weakness."** These words are my *encouragement and strength each day. In* Jesus *name***,** *I pray Amen.*

SELF INFLICTED WOUNDS

We often give the devil too much credit or recognition when bad things happen. While It's convenient to blame the devil, we must also examine ourselves to ensure that we are not to blame for certain things happening in our lives. Yes, it is our self-inflicted wounds.

Do you position the devil within your thoughts to have that much control over your life, or are you employing him through your actions, your choices, or your decisions? Far too many times, we overlook our actions or behaviors, constantly trying to find someone or something to blame for the wrong choices and decisions we sometimes make. Placing the blame elsewhere shows a lack of accountability for our actions.

If you don't discipline your flesh, you give license to the devil to operate freely in your life.

The Bible has already given us a foundation for recognizing or dealing with many self-inflicted wounds we often bring upon ourselves. It speaks about the work of the flesh in **Galatians 5:19-21**, which says:

"Now the works of the flesh are evident, which are: adultery, fornication, uncleanness, lewdness, idolatry, sorcery, hatred, contentions, jealousies, outbursts of wrath, selfish ambitions, dissensions, heresies, envy, murders, drunkenness, revelries, and the like; of which I tell you beforehand, just as I also told you in time past, that those who practice such things will not inherit the kingdom of God."

This is why it's essential to become followers of Christ because if we are following Jesus and listening to His spirit, the devil cannot touch us; therefore, we should think twice before giving credit to the devil for anything happening in our lives, for It is the practice of sinning that invites the devil in. Why not take some time and make a list, then examine your life to see whether it's you or if it is indeed the devil? Don't be surprised if you find out that the devil didn't have anything to do with your situation.

In all probability, it could be more of you and less of him. I know we are quick to give credit to the devil, but the truth is that many of us don't want to discipline ourselves, and so often, we make bad choices or unhealthy decisions. I can truly testify to this statement because when I look back on past situations, most of the negative things that happened in my life were due to my choices or destructive behaviors.

Please understand this. If you don't discipline your flesh, you give license to the devil to operate freely in your life. This is why you must deny your flesh daily. To discipline your life, you have to empower your thinking. Your mind must be conditioned to control the desires of your flesh. It's important to discipline your mind so that the desires of your flesh do not influence your thinking. You always need to be careful and never allow yourself to be subjected to things that are not healthy for your life. You must make wise choices and wise decisions and hold yourself accountable to ensure you are not the root cause of any negativity happening in your life. Self-Inflicted Wounds. Are you the problem, or are you still casting the blame? That's the question.

"Hard work, Consistency, Determination, Faith. If you are praying for greatness, then give God something to work with"

#PrayerDrivenLife

DAILY PRAYERS
AND INSIGHTFUL ENCOURAGEMENTS
WEEK 08

Monday

SCRIPTURE:
Psalm 101:7
He who works deceit shall not dwell within my house; He who tells lies shall not continue in my presence.

Heavenly Father, thank You for giving me grace to stay focus throughout this day. I understand the distractions that has plagued this society is the works of the enemy who seeks to bring much confusion to this world. Father, I pray for peace upon this nation. I pray against the spirit of lies and deceitfulness, and I bind every hindering spirit and I rebuke this wicked behavior that has plagued our nation. I pray for the people of this nation and throughout the world, to restore their hearts to righteousness, and reject that which is not truth. For the enemy has come to steal, kill, destroy, and mislead your people. He has placed in their hearts a false sense of hope that has cause many to stray from the truth. Forgive us Father, for we have brought shame to righteousness through our acceptance and silence towards wickedness. I pray for an end to this influence, I pray for deliverance to come upon a nation that has brought inflictions upon itself. I command every mind to be free! To be released! To be restored and renewed to reject evil and to embrace the righteousness of your words, and allow it to be the foundation in which we all think, being unified, and led by Christ, and not by evil. In Jesus name I pray, Amen!!
2 Peter 3:9, Galatians 5:1, Romans 12:2.

Tuesday

WELCOMING HEART

Every day, love must be a mandate, and neither race nor gender must dictate our ability to love. Who amongst us says we represent Christ but can comfortably sit and watch helpless homeless foreigners, hopelessly looking for a better life in this country, and not allow them to come in? What would Jesus do? What would Christ say? Would he build a wall? Would He use arm guards to sit and watch them suffer? Such actions are not those of our Lord, who loves and welcomes all. For Jesus love is unconditional. He loves without judgment. Even though we were sinners, He paid the ultimate price with His life so we could live. He did not die for a chosen few, but he died for us all, and He commanded from us that we are to love others just as He loves us. Oh ye shameful selfish souls who speak without heart, who want to deny others the same freedom and opportunity that many of your ancestors fled their countries for. The same freedom was granted to many of your ancestors when they suffered the same hardships. This question I ask of you, What if Heaven had a wall? What if Jesus said only those who was denied on earth can come in? What if those who were denied stood at the gates of Heaven, rejecting you who denied them, and now you can't get in? Yes, it's only a hypothetical question, but you must understand that Jesus love surpasses all understanding, and He would never do this to us. His love is pure love above anything we could ever understand, this is why we must practice the same love toward others.

Wednesday

SCRIPTURE:
Proverbs 3:5
Trust in the Lord with all your heart,
And lean not on your own understanding;

Joshua 1:9
Have I not commanded you? Be strong and of good courage; do not be afraid, nor be dismayed, for the Lord your God is with you wherever you go."

It's important to keep life as simple as possible, not allowing distractions or stress to take its hold, but laboring to keep a positive attitude, as well as, keep a positive mindset throughout each day. Life is really not that complicated, but it's mostly depends on how we choose to live life is what often makes life to seem like it's so complicated . . .

Father God, continue to order my steps each day, and strengthen me as I labor to structure my life according to Your principles. Everyday Father, I pray for guidance and wisdom to overcome my failures, and I also pray for corrections through my mistakes. It is my goals Father God, to live life not with my own understanding, but trusting You to order my steps daily, to help me to understand those things that's not clear to me, and most of all, help me to discipline my life. In Jesus name, I pray. Amen

"You've had a purpose in life long before people started having comments about your life. Don't allow negative comments to hinder your purpose."
#PrayerDrivenLife

Thursday

SCRIPTURE:
Romans 12:12
rejoicing in hope, patient in tribulation, continuing steadfastly in prayer;

Romans 8:25
But if we hope for what we do not see, we eagerly wait for it with perseverance.

There is power when we learn to have patience. Sometimes we might not be ready for that next level. We might not be mature enough to take that next step. Having patience is very important because it helps us to hear God, to make wise choices, and to prepare ourselves properly. So often many of us jump into certain things without properly being prepared, but we have to constantly ask ourselves . . . Am I truly ready? Do I have enough tolerance? How thick is my skin when it comes to challenges and criticism? Is my relationship with God strong enough so that I can hear His guidance? We should all have a certain level of patience within ourselves, and we must constantly nurture it daily. The more we learn to exercise patience, the more we learn to trust God, and when we trust God, we can easily trust the process. Let's pray this prayer together . . .

Heavenly Father above all things give me patience. Help me to not be anxious about anything, but to learn patience, and to always hear Your voice above my own thoughts. In Jesus name I pray, Amen. ***Romans 8:25***

Friday

SCRIPTURE:
Philippians 4:19
And my God shall supply all your need according to His riches in glory by Christ Jesus.

Ephesians 6:11
Put on the whole armor of God, that you may be able to stand against the wiles of the devil.

Lord, thank You for preparing me today for whatever life has in store for me. Thank You for encouraging my thinking, for building my character, and for positioning me to approach life in a confident and positive way. I give honor to You Lord for being the source of my strength today. I believe I can do all things through Christ which strengthens me. Today Father, I have victory because of Your presence upon my life. I put on the whole armor of God so that I may be able to stand against the schemes of the devil. I feel more blessed than ever Father, because You constantly favor me. You supply every need concerning me, for this is the assurances that builds my faith knowing that I can always depend on You Father, In Jesus name I pray. Amen. **Philippians 4:13.**

Saturday

SIMPLICITY OF LIFE

The simplicity of life becomes increasingly easier when we learn how to approach life, and how to position ourselves through every encounter we face when we learn patience, and most of all, when we truly understand our identity. Life is not as complicated as we often make it. It only becomes problematic when we don't structure it properly. Join me in praying this prayer . . .

Heavenly Father, thank You for guidance today as You have established my steps throughout this day. By faith, I understand that the power of Your words created the world. Therefore, I stand on Your words each day, hoping to structure my life and help me balance and discipline my life each day. Your word says in **Hebrews 12:11, Now no chastening seems to be joyful for the present, but painful; nevertheless, afterward, it yields the peaceable fruit of righteousness to those trained by it.** Therefore, Father, I open my heart to discipline because it helps me establish stability. In Jesus name, I pray, Amen.

SCRIPTURE:
Proverbs 16:9, Hebrews 11:3, Hebrews 12:11

Sunday

I learned a long time ago about the importance of forgiveness, and how quickly I must position my heart to forgive others even when they have offended me. Forgiveness is not only for the other person, but it's very important for me, because having an unforgiving heart can keep me in bondage, it can cause one to harbor certain emotions that causes them to act out of character. It also causes many distractions within your own mind, which can often hinder your focus. Yes, one can easily feel betrayed or hurt. Yes, it's often puzzling sometimes what people will do or say to you, but you have to ask yourself . . . Is it better to harbor such emotions and loose your peace, or is it better to quickly forgive, and let go and move on with your life having a sense of peace and happiness? . . .

Heavenly Father, Your words says in Proverbs 19:11 ***"The discretion of a man makes him slow to anger, And his glory is to overlook a transgression."*** Help me to always approach any given situation with a forgiving heart. Strengthen me to love beyond my offense, and to never be in bondage by my own ways of reasoning and thinking. I understand the importance of forgiveness, and I pray that each day I am positioned to forgive others, because I know as Your words clearly states in **Matthew 6:14-15** ***"For if you forgive men their trespasses, your heavenly Father will also forgive you. But if you do not forgive men their trespasses, neither will your Father forgive your trespasses."*** That's my encouragement to always forgive no matter how uncomfortable it might feel at that moment. In Jesus name I pray, Amen

"The most important thing I learned about pursuing my dreams, is to understand your purpose before you start pursuing. There is nothing worse than being on a journey you're not destined to be on."

#PrayerDrivenLife

Chapter 08
REPOSITION YOUR HEART

SCRIPTURE REFERENCE
Galatians 5:22-23 Amp.
But the fruit of the Spirit [the result of His presence within us] is love [unselfish concern for others], joy, [inner] peace, patience [not the ability to wait, but how we act while waiting], kindness, goodness, faithfulness, gentleness, self-control. Against such things there is no law.

PRAYER
Heavenly Father, I pray that Your wisdom pours through this message so that all who read it gain knowledge and understanding to position their hearts to be used by You at any given time. In Jesus' name, I pray, amen.

REPOSITION YOUR HEART
As I was preparing to go to Walmart early one morning, the Holy Spirit spoke to me, saying, "*REPOSITION YOUR HEART*," and told me to read **Galatians 5:22**. When I got to the store, just as I started to walk into the door, I noticed this fragile old lady struggling to walk through the door, so I rushed to assist her by opening the manual side door. Still, instead of walking through the door I had already opened for her, she stared at me having this evil expression upon her face, quickly she turned and walked in the other direction towards the automatic doors instead. I immediately recognized the spirit of hate and racism that I discerned from her spirit. Although disappointed by her interaction, I didn't say anything; I just kindly smiled at her and continued with what I had come to the store for. As I searched the store, the Holy Spirit said to me once again, "REPOSITION YOUR HEART," and again told me to read **Galatians 5:22**, so I pulled out my phone and began to read it, but this time, I wrote it down on a piece of paper, and put it in my pocket, as I continued shopping.

As I approached the register to check out, the old lady was already at the cash register. As the cashier completed the checkout of her groceries, I couldn't help but hear the exchanges between the old lady and the cashier. It appeared that she didn't have enough to purchase all her items; she was $25.95 short, and the cashier was trying to help her figure out what she needed to put back. Without any thought whatsoever, I interrupted them and told the cashier to complete the transaction and I would pay the remaining balance. The old lady looked at me and realized that I was the one she had been rude to before, and she asked with a look of guilt on her face, "You would do this for me even after the way I treated you earlier? I did not say a word. I paid the cashier the remaining balance and remained silent with a smile. As the old lady began to walk away, she turned and asked me, "How can I ever repay you for your generosity? Suddenly, I reached into my pocket and gave her the note with the scripture on it from Galatians 5:22, which the Holy Spirit directed me to read earlier as I entered the store. As she reached out for the note, I answered her question, "How can you ever repay me for my generosity? I answered her by saying the same thing the Holy Spirit said to me; "Read the scripture on this note I'm giving you and "REPOSITION YOUR HEART". . .

The old lady looked down at the paper, feeling just as confused about what that meant as I did when the Holy Spirit said it to me. I told her to read the note I had given her, and if she were sincerely grateful, her heart would receive the message on the note. As she began to walk away, she glimpsed back at me after carefully reading the note and appeared to display a pleasant smile on her face while reading the note. As she continued to move towards the exit, she stopped several times and read the scripture I had given her, and each time, she smiled as if the scripture had prompted a change in her heart. I felt grateful afterward because I positioned myself through God's word to allow the Holy Spirit to use me.

I realized it was because of my obedience when the Holy Spirit told me to reposition my heart. I was positioned to do God's will at the right time as the situation prompted me to deliver the message to its target. More and more, as we labor in God's words, it's essential to understand how to position our hearts to hear God and to seek wisdom daily. We must also learn how to apply His principles to our daily lives to be prepared for every encounter. God's words teach us the correct way to approach certain situations, which can often be beyond our understanding.

Often, we will encounter hatred and racism. There should never be any tolerance for those who harbor such evil in their hearts because we are all created by the same God, and He did not discriminate in His creations of us, yet we were created equal for a divine purpose to glorify and please Him. This is why we must wear the characteristics of the fruit of the spirit because you never know where your blessing might come from or who God might be positioning you to bless.
REPOSITION YOUR HEART!

"Oftentimes the only thing people need to know about you, is that you exist, and even that is sometimes too much of your business to put out. It's ok to be a MYSTERY"

#PrayerDrivenLife

DAILY PRAYERS AND INSIGHTFUL ENCOURAGEMENTS WEEK 09

Monday

SCRIPTURE:
Colossians 3:2-5
Set your mind on things above, not on things on the earth. For you died, and your life is hidden with Christ in God. When Christ who is our life appears, then you also will appear with Him in glory. Therefore put to death your members which are on the earth: fornication, uncleanness, passion, evil desire, and covetousness, which is idolatry.

I can recall early one Monday morning, I became so preoccupied mentally, totally exhausted in my thoughts simply because I changed my daily routine of preparing for my day through meditation and prayer each morning as I awaken. It sort of made me realize how important it is for my mindset to be my greatest priority each day, because it's the most vulnerable part of me that must be nurtured at all times. The mind is certainly a place that's often invaded. Its a place which must be constantly guarded even from my own thoughts which is often my biggest influence. Let us pray this prayer . . .

Heavenly Father, help me to keep my mind focus each day, to establish Your words as my thoughts in order to find comfort and rest in your presence as I continue to keep my mind set on the things that are above, and not on the things of this earth. In Jesus name I pray Amen.

Tuesday

THE POWER OF BEING GOD-FOCUSED

The greatest FOCUS I can have is on God, to understand who I am in Christ Jesus and to work daily to improve me so that God can effectively use me. Who am I to judge others when I am always a work in progress? Who am I to question the calling on someone else's life when I have yet to fulfill or completely understand the calling on my life? What gives me the right to criticize others but allow myself to go without corrections? When I learn to FOCUS ON IMPROVING ME. I have very little room to criticize or judge others. Am I so self-righteous that I have forgotten how jacked up I was before Jesus saved me? Have I not remembered the mistakes I've made to get to the place I'm at today? How dare I put my mouth on others as if I have arrived? Shame on me for turning my FOCUS from myself and directing it towards others while I am still a work in progress. This is why FOCUSING on IMPROVING myself is so important because there's so much of me that needs discipline, so much of God's word I need in me to help me to grow, to prepare me for my calling, and most of all, to structure my life in ways I can genuinely be consistent in my calling. Once again, I say to myself . . . THE GREATEST FOCUS I CAN HAVE IN LIFE IS IMPROVING MYSELF!

Wednesday

SCRIPTURE:
Psalm 28:7
The Lord is my strength and my shield; My heart trusted in Him, and I am helped; Therefore my heart greatly rejoices, And with my song I will praise Him.

Philippians 4:13
I can do all things through Christ who strengthens me.

Heavenly Father, You are my strength and my shield; in You my heart trusts, and I am helped; my heart exults, and with my song I give thanks and praises to You. Thank You Father for life today, thank You for this feeling of joy that gives me so much comfort and rest. I believe today that I can do all things through Christ Jesus which strengthens me. Thank You Father for giving me the confidence to conquer this day, for my heart and mind You have empowered though meditation and prayer. Father today I decree favor and blessing upon the lives of everyone who receives this prayer, with hopes that on this day, prosperity and success shall be with them, and it is my prayer that they shall fulfill the purpose of their day, In Jesus name I pray, Amen ,

"I discovered something a long time ago. The devil needed my help in order to destroy me, so I stopped helping him."
#PrayerDrivenLife

Thursday

SCRIPTURE:
1Corinthians 9:27
But I discipline my body and bring it into subjection, lest, when I have preached to others, I myself should become disqualified.

Hebrews 12:11, Matthew 29:18, Acts 1:8.

I thank You Heavenly Father everyday for deliverance. I thank You for choosing my path, for opening my ears and heart to receive Your words which changes my life. Father, I'm grateful that You love me, you sustain me through the most difficult times. Thank You for giving me the strength to stay consistent in my calling, to hear Your voice, and to fulfill every task You put before me each day. Father, I pray for a stronger relationship with You, to hear You even more, and to avoid the influences of this world. Teach me everyday Father to focus above my distractions, prepare me to impact others in ways that brings them closer to You. Search my heart each day Father, and help me to remove anything in me that hinders my growth. Prepare me for discipleship, to teach your words, to heal the sick and bring deliverance to those who have lost their way. Father, everyday I understand that I am a work in progress, constantly open to corrections and discipline. I pray that no parts of me be left without change for the greater good of fulfilling Your purpose for my life. In Jesus name I pray, Amen.

Friday

SCRIPTURE:
Colossians 3: 14-17
But above all these things put on love, which is the bond of perfection. And let the peace of God rule in your hearts, to which also you were called in one body; and be thankful. Let the word of Christ dwell in you richly in all wisdom, teaching and admonishing one another in psalms and hymns and spiritual songs, singing with grace in your hearts to the Lord. And whatever you do in word or deed, do all in the name of the Lord Jesus, giving thanks to God the Father through Him.

Heavenly Father, thank You for positioning my heart today, for strengthening my mind to think positive and be filled with the confessions of Words. You are a great and mighty presence in my life each day, I look forward to my time with You. I worship Your name, I lift up my voice singing praises to Your name, for Your presence upon my life is a reflection of the joy I feel each day. Father, I'm grateful that You love me without conditions. I'm grateful for our Lord and savor Jesus Christ, for His blood covers me, and restores me each day. For He paid the ultimate price for my sins. Thank You Father for covering my family, my friends, and everyone who receives this prayer today. I speak blessings and healing upon their lives. I decree favor upon their lives, with hopes that success shall follow them throughout this day. In Jesus name I pray, Amen.

Saturday

SCRIPTURE:
James 1:4-8

*But let patience have its perfect work, that you may be perfect and complete, lacking nothing. If any of you lacks wisdom, let him ask of God, who gives to all liberally and without reproach, and it will be given to him. But let him ask in faith, with no doubting, for he who doubts is like a wave of the sea driven and tossed by the wind. For let not that man suppose that he will receive anything from the Lord; **8** he is a double-minded man, unstable in all his ways..*

Life without patience, is often a life without peace, and a life filled with mistakes. How many times can you truly say that being impatience has benefited you? . . .

Heavenly Father, help me to not be anxious about anything concerning my life, but let patience have its perfect work so that I may be perfect and complete not lacking anything. Forgive me Father, for trying to do things my own way. Forgive me for my lack of trust in You, for my impatience has in many ways blind my judgement, but I understand that there is no better corrections than Your wisdom which guides my life. In Jesus name I pray Amen.

Sunday

SCRIPTURE:
Deuteronomy 20:4.
for the Lord your God is He who goes with you, to fight for you against your enemies, to save you.'

You can have good days, or you can have bad days. Whichever one you have today will often depend on how you respond to the challenges that awaits you today. The devil is ready for you today. The question is . . . Are you prepared to make him irrelevant or ineffective today? Are you focus? Have you taken the necessary steps to position your mind? What is your level of tolerance today? . . . .

Heavenly Father, thank You for preparing me for this day, for positioning my mindset to be focus on You, and to know my purpose and defeat any distractions that comes before me. I am grateful for Your words which empowers my confessions, which gives me hope and encourages me throughout each day. In Jesus name I pray, Amen.

"You have to help people with a heart conditioned with LOVE, because the very ones you've helped so often will freely cut you off, but because your heart is positioned to LOVE, it doesn't change your heart, it preserves the kindness of your spirit"

#PrayerDrivenLife

Chapter 09
THE IMPORTANCE OF PATIENCE

SCRIPTURE REFERENCE
JAMES 1:4-5
But let patience have its perfect work, that you may be [a]perfect and complete, lacking nothing. If any of you lacks wisdom, let him ask of God, who gives to all liberally and without reproach, and it will be given to him.

PRAYER
Father God, I pray for patience each day, to not be anxious for anything, but to allow things to manifest and to keep me in alignment with You Father God. Let your patience live in me, Father, and strengthen me to wait on you, to approach all things having wisdom and understanding to make wise decisions. It is my desire, Father God, to let patience have its perfect work so that I may be perfect and complete, lacking nothing. In Jesus name, I pray, Amen.

THE IMPORTANCE OF PATIENCE
How often have you said that you're going to wait on God but then turn around and do whatever you want to do anyway? I myself have done so more times than I can remember, only to learn the hard way that It takes a lot of patience and restraint to wait on God, because He operates in His timing. God knows what's best for us more than we know ourselves; therefore, it's best to wait patiently for Him instead of trying to do things our way. Making decisions for your life can often be challenging, but the most important thing you can do when making life-changing decisions is to put it before God first, then pray, and wait until He gives you peace to make the right decisions. Waiting on God requires much patience, and with such patience, you can develop a level of maturity that prevents you from hindering your life's journey.

I have to admit I've failed so often throughout my life, trying to do things my way, but in doing things my way, it hasn't always been what was best for me. My choices have always made connections with questionable people with no character or integrity. Developing patience has truly helped me to make wise decisions. Being able to hear God more, has rooted me in knowledge, and it has prepared me in ways which makes it easier to navigate life without too many complications. And I credit patience for always keeping me grounded.

Every day, I pray for patience. I pray for wisdom to know when to sit still and wait on God's timing, so that it helps me to make good decisions for my life. Believe me, as I say this: none of us are immune to mistakes, and neither can we escape the challenges of the devil who constantly tries to reap habit in our lives. Still, as we develop patience, we gain much-needed wisdom to defend ourselves against the works of the enemy.

As I have become older, my desire for peace grows stronger everyday, and patience helps me to establish peace mentally. It's the most valuable tool in my possession. It strengthens my mind as I become less distracted, because I'm learning to let go and let God. Take a moment and look back at all the bad situations you've been through. You can see now how some things could have been avoided by having patience. I want to leave you with this question to ponder. How many of you can truly say being impatient has benefited you?

"Everyone has a LIFE to live, a PURPOSE to fulfill, and a JOURNEY to travel. Once you truly understand that, and truly start to focus on you, then maybe . . . Just maybe, you'll be less critical of others"

#PrayerDrivenLife

DAILY PRAYERS AND INSIGHTFUL ENCOURAGEMENTS WEEK 10

Monday

SCRIPTURE:
John 13:34-35
A new commandment I give to you, that you love one another: just as I have loved you, you also are to love one another. By this all people will know that you are my disciples, if you have love for one another."

1 John 4:16
So we have come to know and to believe the love that God has for us. God is love, and whoever abides in love abides in God, and God abides in him.

Father, I am forever grateful for the love I often feel in my heart. You constantly show me how to love others by always being my example of what true love is. Teach me to love just as Jesus has always loved us. Even as others have wrong me, help me to love past any anger or hurt, always being quick to forgive and slow to respond through emotional responses. Thank You Lord for always being patience with me, and it is my prayers that You will help me to be patience with others, never to walk in judgement of anyone, but understand that we all struggle with something in our lives daily. Father, today I humble myself with love, I position myself to love, and most of all, I strive to be just like Jesus, who is truly the greatest love we've ever encountered. In Jesus name I pray, Amen!

Tuesday

APPRECIATE YOURSELF

Today, I encourage you always to appreciate who you are and value the greatness that lives inside of you because no matter how much you do for others, they will never see your value as you see it in yourself. You must always be encouraged and know that God has gifted you to be great. You must learn to stay humble and not get discouraged when you are overlooked or feel less appreciated because your purpose is more significant than your current state. God is creating an economy in you that will sustain you and be more beneficial than any appreciation or gratitude ever will. He's perfecting your craft so the world can see and know you are His child. So, continue to stay obedient to your assignments. You must understand that there's a greater purpose in store for you when helping others succeed. YOUR DESTINY and YOUR PURPOSE will be greatly fulfilled because of your obedience and sacrifices. This is why I want to encourage each of you, as I even encourage myself, to keep your mind focused on the PURPOSE of your journey, and not the process, because after the process, and after all you've had to endure, GREATNESSES will surely manifest!!

Wednesday

SCRIPTURE:
Isaiah 26:3
You will keep him in perfect peace, Whose mind is stayed on You, Because he trusts in You.

Heavenly Father, May Your grace and protection be upon my life throughout this day, giving me strength where I am weak, giving me wisdom to make the best decisions for my life. Thank You for healing my body and for renewing my mind each day. Thank You for empowering my thoughts as I meditate on Your words each day. Your words brings life and encouragement, it shelters me from my emotions and it brings stability to my thinking. **Isaiah 26:3 says: "You will keep him in perfect peace, Whose mind is stayed on You, Because he trusts in You."** Yes Father, my trust is always in You. In Jesus name I pray, Amen

"If you don't won't to learn, then don't knock the person that's teaching. Knowledge is power! You're never too old to learn something new, to gain a greater understanding of how to improve your mindset. That doesn't happen without knowledge."
#PrayerDrivenLife

Thursday

STRENGTHEN YOUR CHARACTER

As I awakened early one morning, the Lord spoke to me and said, "Strengthen your character with silence."
Suddenly, I realized how much I had to learn to absorb certain things I heard without always responding. We often allow our emotions to get the best of us, which often causes us to act out of character. Like many of you, I know I'm not perfect, but the character of who I am is something I work so hard to improve on daily. People will often test your character with conversations, and if you are not wise in responding to them, you can say things or do things completely opposite to your character. This is why the word says in ***James 1:19, "So then, my beloved brethren, let every man be swift to hear, slow to speak, slow to wrath;*** I'm learning every day how important it is to guard my hearing, to never approach any situation emotionally, but with an open mind to process what I hear and respond to it with the greatest amount of wisdom. How can we grow and improve without constantly searching and evaluating ourselves daily? Every day, I am a work in progress; the character of who I am must continuously be aligned with the character of who Jesus is. Indeed, I will often fail many times. Indeed, people will often judge me harshly, but my only concern in life is not what people think of me but how often I'm growing and Improving my life to create a better and more beautiful me!

Friday

SCRIPTURE:
Colossians 3:16
Let the word of Christ dwell in you richly in all wisdom, teaching and admonishing one another in psalms and hymns and spiritual songs, singing with grace in your hearts to the Lord.

Jeremiah 33:6
Behold, I will bring it health and healing; I will heal them and reveal to them the abundance of peace and truth.

Heavenly Father, thank You for Your grace and protection over us all, as we journey out into the world today. I pray for stability in this nation, with hopes that common sense overrule selfish ideologies. I pray for healing for those who are suffering both mentally and physically, as You send Your words and healed them. Thank You Father, for the blood of Jesus which covers us daily. Thank you for guidance and instructions, as we all strive to conquer life, while learning to love one another each and every day, while also striving to fulfill the assignments You have giving each of us. In Jesus name, today I surrender my will, so that Your will be done through me, Amen. ***Psalm 32:8***

Saturday

SCRIPTURE:
Proverbs 4:23
Keep your heart with all diligence, For out of it spring the issues of life.

Matthew 5:8
Blessed are the pure in heart, For they shall see God.

The heart is the most important part of our body which is often targeted by the enemy daily. It can often harbor many things. It can be pure and often filled with sincerity. It can be loving, but at times, it can be filled with hate, or rage. The heart can often show compassion and love, but many times it can become waxed cold totally influencing our emotions . . .

Heavenly Father, help me to keep my heart pure, and totally guided by you. Examine my heart as well as my thoughts each day and remove anything that's not aligned with you. Father, I understand that love is the most powerful thing one can posses in their heart each day. Help me to keep my heart filled with love and compassion, and labor to keep it guarded at all times. In Jesus name I pray, Amen

Sunday

SCRIPTURE:
John 14:3
And if I go and prepare a place for you, I will come again and receive you to Myself; that where I am, there you may be also.

What good is life if you can't enjoy it. What good is life if you don't appreciate it. What good is life if you can't see the true value of it. What good is life without Jesus. . . .

Heavenly Father, thank you for the precious gift of life, and for making it easy for me to live efficiently each day. There's often so much joy in my life because of You Father, and I appreciate how You constantly watch over me and my family daily. Because of the sacrifices Jesus made for us, I truly value life, and the things you delivered me from. I have to look forward to each day, knowing that there is a place prepared for me, a life of eternal happiness. That's the hope that keeps my mind at peace. In Jesus name I pray. Amen.

"Sometimes you just have to praise the Lord, and rest in Him, and block out everything happening around you and trust God through it all. Do you trust me? Yes Lord, I trust You with every area of my life."

#PrayerDrivenLife

Chapter 10
MY JOURNEY TO OVERCOME DEPRESSION

SCRIPTURE REFERENCE
ISAIAH 26:3
You keep him in perfect peace whose mind is stayed on you, because he trusts in you.

COLOSSIANS 3:2
Set your mind on things above, not on things on the earth.

PRAYER
Heavenly Father, restore my mind each day, let your peace be upon my life, and keep me out of harm's way. Help me, Father God, to always keep my thoughts pure, to keep my mind focused on You, the source of my peace. In Jesus' name, I pray, amen.

OVERCOMING DEPRESSION
Whenever I see someone going through depression, I can relate to their struggles because of my past experiences with depression. The spirit of depression is something one should never take lightly. It could easily alter your mindset and overwhelm you with emotions and feelings beyond your control. Have you ever felt those feelings within, making you feel like no one understands you? Are you constantly having feelings of anxiety and feelings of emptiness that hinder your ability to communicate with anyone? Once depression gets its hold on you, it becomes difficult to free yourself from its grip. There's one thing that I learned about depression: it can cause you to become emotionally drained, and it also creates unhealthy thoughts, which gives you a false illusion. More and more each day, as I began to search within myself for answers as to why I was feeling so depressed, I began to evaluate my mindset, and this is when I discovered my depression was self-inflicted. Yes, that's right, it was because of my thinking and

how I would process things mentally. For this reason, God's word becomes so crucial because it helps us to discipline our minds. If you don't learn to discipline your life, as well as your mindset, you can easily give license to the enemy to invade your mind in ways that can cause you to destroy yourself mentally, and it will also cause you to ruin your relationship with everyone around you.

I knew that to overcome depression, first, I had to overcome ME. Yes, that's right, I had to overcome myself above all things. I understood It was my thinking that caused my depression because I didn't know how to let go and move on beyond my disappointments. The devil always targets our minds. He knows if he can cause us to become preoccupied with negative thoughts, we could quickly lose control of ourselves. The spirit of depression is powerful; it lures you into a state of sadness, and it smothers every ounce of happiness within you with the hope of isolating you from others. Learning to channel my focus through God's word gave me hope during difficult times. It helped me to overcome that stronghold of depression. I can't imagine how anyone who chooses to live without the presence of God in their life could overcome such a mighty stronghold, but I thank God for His word. As I began to lean on *1 Peter 5:7*, which says: *"casting all your care upon Him, for He cares for you"*, I started to trust God more. His word was the confidence I needed, and as I began to meditate on His words daily, it became easier to control my thoughts by bringing them under the submission of God's word. Just like it says in *Isaiah 26:3*, *"You will keep him in perfect peace, Whose mind is stayed on You, Because he trusts in You."* And also, *Romans 8:6 says: "For to be carnally minded is death, but to be spiritually minded is life and peace."* You can't allow negativity to be a part of your thought process. You have to learn to feed your mind daily and to do so, that takes a commitment, as well as faith and patience.

Life will always have challenges, but there is hope to overcome them when you have faith in God and trust that He will never leave or forsake you. This type of mindset has always been my motivation against depression. As I began to lean on God's words, I started to trust in God more and understand His promises and His words became my daily confession. I started replacing negative thoughts with positive confessions. I changed my outlook on life and allowed my faith to dictate my responses. As soon as I made this commitment to draw near to God and lean on Him, my mindset became free, and depression no longer had its grip on me. I developed this renewed mindset, which helped me to defeat the spirit of depression. I had to understand the power that lives inside of me and to know who I am and whom I belong to. I've always had to be prepared for warfare and its assignment against my life. The devil wants to destroy us all, and he often targets our minds, looking for ways to weaken us with our thoughts, but God's word is our shield. It's our bread of life, and we must feed off of it daily. We must understand Its power and keep it deep within our hearts, and by doing so, it will always be our protector.

"If you really want to be amazing today . . . Pray for someone who needs prayer. Encourage someone who needs encouragement. Love on someone who needs love."
#PrayerDrivenLife

DAILY PRAYERS
AND INSIGHTFUL ENCOURAGEMENTS
WEEK 11

Monday

SCRIPTURE:
Hebrews 10:35-36
Therefore do not cast away your confidence, which has great reward. For you have need of endurance, so that after you have done the will of God, you may receive the promise:

Heavenly Father, thank You for the blessings of this day, for guiding me throughout another week with patience and endurance to deal with any challenges that's awaiting me. Help me to align my thoughts with Your words. Help me to keep a positive prospective on life despite everything happening in this world. My desire everyday is to hear You, to structure my life according to Your words, to live each day in peace, totally aligned with Your designed purpose for my life. In Jesus name I pray. Amen.

Tuesday

SCRIPTURE:
Hebrews 10:35-36
And Jesus said to him, "Assuredly, I say to you, today you will be with Me in Paradise."

2 Corinthians 1:3-4
Blessed *be* the God and Father of our Lord Jesus Christ, the Father of mercies and God of all comfort, who comforts us in all our tribulation, that we may be able to comfort those who are in any trouble, with the comfort with which we ourselves are comforted by God.

It's always difficult when you loose a love one, or when you loose a friend suddenly. Death is a part of life that's not easy to adjust to, but death and life is in God's hands. It's a calling, a journey to a place of everlasting peace for those who love the Lord. The word says in ***Ezekiel 18:4 "Behold, all souls are mine", and in Luke 23:43 "Truly, I say to you, today you will be with me in Paradise."*** . . .

Heavenly Father, thank You for life, for bringing comfort to those who have lost their love ones. Please bring peace and healing to their hearts throughout this process. In Jesus name I pray Amen.

Wednesday

SCRIPTURE:
Hebrews 12:1
Therefore we also, since we are surrounded by so great a cloud of witnesses, let us lay aside every weight, and the sin which so easily ensnares us, and let us run with endurance the race that is set before us,

Ephesians 5:15-16
See then that you walk circumspectly, not as fools but as wise, redeeming the time, because the days are evil.

Many times our past experiences can often be the reason why we respond to, or how we deal with certain situations. Life only repeats itself if we constantly do the same thing without making adjustments. It's always important not to be so quick to blame others when we find ourselves in a repeated cycle. The best decision we can ever make is to examine our own actions first to see if we can eliminate ourselves as being the root cause of any problem we face. This can better empower one to make better decisions . . .

Heavenly Father, empower me to make the best decisions in life, to always examine myself for corrections and improvements. In Jesus name I pray, Amen

"It doesn't matter how much you think you know, or how smart you think you are, there is still a lot more to learn when it comes to life. As long as you breathe LIFE, you will be a student of life."

#PrayerDrivenLife

Thursday

SCRIPTURE:
Matthew 19:26
But Jesus looked at them and said to them, "With men this is impossible, but with God all things are possible."

Mark 9:23
Jesus said to him, "If you can believe, all things are possible to him who believes."

Having confidence and believing in yourself is easy when you understand who you are in Christ Jesus. Many of us fail to tap into our potential, because we are often overcome by distractions. But our relationship with Jesus gives us confidence and hope, believing that we can do all things through Him, and it is Christ Himself who initiates the experience of the supernatural which greatly empowers us to succeed . . .

Lord Jesus, Thank You for helping me to know who I am, and for guiding me. Thank You for being the greatest example to follow in life. Because of Your sacrifices, I truly believe I can achieve greatness in life, and nothing can prohibit my success but me. In Jesus name, Amen
Philippians 4:13,

Friday

SCRIPTURE:
Isaiah 26:3
You will keep him in perfect peace, Whose mind is stayed on You, Because he trusts in You.

When my mind is free, and my thoughts are pure, my days are often less stressful . . .

Heavenly Father, thank You for empowering my mind each day, and for awaking me each morning fully prepared for my journey throughout this day. Today, I am focus, as my confessions are filled with empowerment, and encouraging words, I believe that I can do all things through Christ which strengthens me. Father, I trust you to provide protection over my life today, to keep me from distractions, even from my own thoughts when they are not in line with You. Thank You Father for freedom, freedom to be me, freedom to be the person You have destine in me. In Jesus name I pray, Amen.
Isaiah 26:3

Saturday

THE POWER TO ACHIEVE

You can be anything you want to be. You can do anything you set your mind to do as long as you believe in yourself. Every one of us has been empowered with a gift. There is an economy inside us waiting to be discovered by you if only you take the time to know your capabilities. What is it that drives you? What are those things you feel most passionate about in life? What are things you find that you are great at doing or making? knowing the answer to these questions should empower you to strive for greatness.

Every day, you must trust your instincts and find motivation within yourself to know that greatness lives in you. You must believe without doubts and confess from your mouth that "I can do all things through Christ Jesus, which strengthens me." You have to believe there are no limits to success except those limits we often place within our minds. There is an economy that lives in each of us. It would help if you separated your gifts from freeloaders and those who want something for nothing and connect with those who genuinely value your gift and see it as a means to sustain your existence. You must explore yourself, explore every ounce of your potential, and prioritize exercising your skills until they bring you independence.

Sunday

SCRIPTURE:
Psalm 118:8
It is better to trust in the Lord Than to put confidence in man.

It doesn't matter what's going on in our lives today, God knows all, and He has equipped you for the challenges of this day. No worries, no complaints, just the blessings of living life, and trusting God at all times . . .

Heavenly Father, I am grateful for Your protection surrounding me today, and for giving me grace to navigate life throughout each day. Today I believe that the favor of your blessings are upon me, and everything I set out to do is achievable. Father God, I trust You with all my heart, above all people and all things, because Your words says in Psalm 118:8 "*It is better to trust in the Lord Than to put confidence in man.*" Therefore I trust in you, and only you Father God, In Jesus name I pray, Amen.

"No matter what situations you're facing, let PEACE guide your responses. PEACE doesn't eliminate your situation, but it gives you the ability to endure through it, and It helps you to sit still and trust God."

#PrayerDrivenLife

Chapter 11
GOD REALIGNED MY BEHAVIOR TO IMPROVE MY FINANCIAL STABILITY

I used to always pray for my finances and for certain things that I wanted out of life, and I paid tithes and sowed financial seeds, hoping that would bring stability to my finances, but very little resulted from any of it, and even when it did, it was gone as quick as it came. Before we begin this chapter, let me make one thing perfectly clear, this chapter is not a discussion against paying tithes and offerings, but i'm strictly speaking about the behavior I once had concerning my finances that kept me in bondage for many years. It wasn't until early one Wednesday morning the Holy Spirit awakened me and spoke these words . . .

" DISCIPLINE, PATIENCE, RESTRAINT, and WISDOM "

I immediately started searching for scriptures and meditating and praying daily concerning these words. Nearly a year had passed, and nothing seemed to change concerning my finances or my life after that visitation from the Holy Spirit that morning, but I consistently stayed the course, trusting and believing that God had led me to study and pray for **discipline**, **patience**, **restraint**, and **wisdom**. As time passed, I gradually began to see changes in my behavior towards my finances. I received several raises from my job in one year, and other raises proceeded afterward in the same manner. I was no longer living from paycheck to paycheck. Still, each pay period, I began seeing a surplus as I became more DISCIPLINE in managing my finances, paying my bills on time, and living within my means while saving more money and spending less, as much as possible. I noticed how I was developing more PATIENCE and I became less anxious about buying certain things while staying clear of a lot of debt, learning to wait on God until He gave me peace in how I would spend my money. It became so easy for me to show RESTRAINT, staying clear of things I didn't need. This helped me simplify my lifestyle and be thankful for what I already had.

Most importantly, God has taught me much-needed wisdom on managing my credit and finances while showing me how to enjoy life without exhausting my resources. He helped me establish a prayer life, teaching me to pray His words, and often led me to scriptures to meditate on daily. After two years of following God's instructions to realign my behavior, I went from a 450 credit score to a 750 credit score. I bought three cars in one year and never missed a payment; neither was I struggling to pay for them. I Qualified for a $340,000 mortgage loan and accumulated over $85,000 worth of available credit, yet through it all, I've never attempted to abuse or misuse any of it. This is a testimony of how God realigned my life and changed my behavior toward my finances over such a short time.

I thank God every day that He intervened in my life and put me on the right track financially. Although my life is still a work in progress, I struggle less financially and no longer live from paycheck to paycheck. So often, we are taught that paying tithes and sowing seeds is all you need to better your life financially, but I found out the hard way that this is far from the truth. It takes more than just paying tithes and sowing seeds. We also have to deal with the biggest hindrance to our financial stability: YOU! Yes, that's right! I said It! It's YOU, and until you learn how to address your behavior and how you deal with your finances, you will continue to struggle financially. The benefits of paying tithes and offerings will become useless without financial discipline.

I realized when the Holy Spirit awakened me and instructed me with these words: **DISCIPLINE, PATIENCE, RESTRAINT,** and **WISDOM**, it prompted me to study the scriptures, and by doing so, God's words begin to change my behaviors, and I became much wiser in managing my behavior towards my finances. Our behavior can often be one of our biggest problems regarding managing our finances.

Don't get me wrong, I am not discrediting sowing or tithing, but we teach so much about paying our tithes and sowing financial seeds; we neglect that many people are irresponsible when handling their finances. I, myself, was one of them. No matter how often I gave, there was no sustainability because I mishandled my finances whenever God blessed me. What good is it to reap a harvest and mismanage it? If you can't handle the least of what you have, you will surely not be able to manage and sustain your increases.

I believe God realigned my priorities because I was undisciplined. My behavior towards my finances had become far too extreme. I rarely paid my bills on time, constantly living beyond my means. How could God trust me, out of all people, to make wise decisions when managing my finances? But today, I can sincerely testify that my life has improved. I'm less stressed, able to do things, and go places I couldn't afford to go before God helped me change my behavior towards my finances. Listen, saints, it's not as complicated as you think it is once you get your behavior under control. There's no greater tool than God's word to challenge yourself and discipline your life if you are willing to commit to it consistently. Notice when I say CONSISTENTLY. One can never be successful without consistency. Like I was, some of you have been paying your tithes and sowing seeds faithfully for years but still struggle. You can't expect God to bless you simply because of that. He has to know that you are prepared and ready to manage your blessings; therefore, your behavior must change just as well. Changing your behavior means dealing with a lot of those things inside of us that keep us in bondage, and that includes learning how to become more disciplined, learning to show restraint, and avoiding those spontaneous actions that cause us to go above what we can afford. Imagine how changing your behavior will realign your lifestyle for the better. It is my prayer that testimony inspire you to realign your behavior towards your finances.

DISCIPLINE, PATIENCE, RESTRAINT, and WISDOM

Throughout my journey of realigning my behavior, many of these scriptures I have included below became part of my daily meditation and prayers. God's word is so important, and it's the greatest tool in helping you to become more disciplined and obedient to His words. Prayer and knowledge changes things for the better, and I pray this powerful testimony encourages you to change your behavior toward your finances and get you on a path to financial stability.

DISCIPLINE
Hebrews 12:1-2, 2 Timothy 2:15, 1 Thessalonians 5:6-8, Colossians 2:23, Philippians 4:8, Philippians 1:27, 1 Corinthians 6:19, Romans 12:3, Romans 8:13, Proverbs 25:28, 1 John 2:15-16, 1 Peter 5:8, 2 Timothy 2:3-4, 2 Corinthians 10:3-5, Romans 13:12-14, Luke 14:27, Philippians 3:12-14, 1 Peter 2:23-24, Colossians 3:5, Galatians 5:23-24, 1 Corinthians 9:24-27, Romans 5:3-5, Isaiah 1:19, Proverbs 15:32, Proverbs 20:13, Hebrews 12:5-11, 2 Timothy 1:7, Titus 1:8, Hebrews 12:11, Proverbs 12:1, Proverbs 3:11-12, Proverbs 25:28

PATIENCE
Revelation 2:19, Revelation 2:3, 2 Timothy 2:24, 2 Thessalonians 3:5, 2 Thessalonians 1:3-5, Nehemiah 9:30, 1 Peter 3:20, 2 Corinthians 6:4-6, Romans 15:4-5, Romans 9:22, Romans 2:7-8, Ecclesiastes 7:8,

Proverbs 16:32, Psalm 40:1, James 1:19-20, Hebrews 6:15-20, 2 Timothy 3:10, 1 Thessalonians 5:14, 1 Corinthians 13:7, Joel 2:13, Psalm 37:7, Colossians 1:11-12, Luke 21:19, Luke 18:7, 1 Peter 2:20-23, Hebrews 12:3, Romans 2:4, James 5:7-10, James 1:2-4, Ephesians 4:2-3, Colossians 3:12-15, Galatians 5:22-23, 1 Corinthians 13:4-5

WISDOM
James 3:13Proverbs 15:33, Colossians 4:5-6, Proverbs 4:11, James 3:17, Proverbs 9:10, Isaiah 28:29, Proverbs 3:13, Romans 11:33, Proverbs 13:20, Isaiah 55:8, Proverbs 2:6 , Proverbs 13:10, Ephesians 5:15-16, Proverbs 16:16, Proverbs 19:8, Proverbs 17:28, 1 Corinthians 3:18, Proverbs 2:6, James 1:5, Proverbs 1:7, 2 Thessalonians 2:10-12, 1 Corinthians 3:18-20, 1 Corinthians 2:13-14, Proverbs 16:25, James 4:10, James 3:13-17, 2 Corinthians 10:5, John 3:27, Proverbs 8:13, Proverbs 3:7, Proverbs 2:1-5, Philippians 2:3, Proverbs 11:2

RESTRAINT
James 3:2, 1 Corinthians 7:5, Colossians 3:14, Ephesians 5:21, Ephesians 4:31-32, James 5:8-11, Hebrews 12:1-2, Galatians 5:16, Proverbs 4:23-27, Proverbs 4:23-27, Galatians 5:13, Matthew 5:5, Isaiah 53:7, Proverbs 16:32, Philippians 2:5, 1 Corinthians 9:24-27, Titus 2:12, Titus 2:6-10, 1 John 2:15, Romans 8:12-13, Proverbs 25:28, 1 Corinthians 9:27, James 1:13-15, 2 Timothy 3:1-3, Proverbs 29:18, Colossians 3:12-13, Ephesians 4:1-3, Galatians 5:22-25

DAILY PRAYERS
AND INSIGHTFUL ENCOURAGEMENTS
WEEK 12

Monday

SCRIPTURE:
Hebrews 12:11
Now no chastening seems to be joyful for the present, but painful; nevertheless, afterward it yields the peaceable fruit of righteousness to those who have been trained by it.

Proverbs 25:28
Whoever has no rule over his own spirit Is like a city broken down, without walls.

We should never be afraid to challenge ourselves as often as we can. The biggest obstacle we often face is the one we see in the mirror. Being successful in life often requires a lot of discipline and a willingness to make tough decisions to address things about ourselves that often hinders our growth. For many of us, this in itself, can often become a very challenging task . . .

Heavenly Father, help me to discipline my life daily, and to overcome the challenges of improving me, but most of all, help me to align my life according to Your purpose, in Jesus name. Amen

Tuesday

A PEACEFUL HEART

Many times, I often try to keep my heart in a peaceful place to avoid being affected by anyone I encounter each day. The society we live in today is filled with selfish-minded people, and no matter how often you try to approach life with a positive attitude, there's always something or someone looking to exploit your peace with negativity. I must keep my mind focused on God and my purpose. I have to approach each day knowing that distractions might come. I understand that offense must come, and my patience might often be tested. Still, even though these things might occur, I cannot just sit idle and allow any attack against my existence. I must continue to speak positive confessions into my environment. I must always keep my heart and thoughts pure because this is when I become most effective in achieving what God has anointed me to do!

SCRIPTURE:
John 14:27
Peace I leave with you, My peace I give to you; not as the world gives do I give to you. Let not your heart be troubled, neither let it be afraid.

Wednesday

SCRIPTURE:
Ephesians 5:16-7
redeeming the time, because the days are evil. Therefore do not be unwise, but understand what the will of the Lord is

Father, help me to manage my time efficiently throughout this week, as each day, I learn to be patient with the process of fulfilling my purpose. I believe that I can do all things through Christ which strengthens me, and no weapons formed against me can defeat my purpose, neither can it hinder my success. Today , I stand on the promises of Your words. I operate without fear, having confidence knowing that You control all things concerning my life. For it is You Father God who gives me power to obtain wealth. That's the confidence which empowers my life daily. In Jesus name I pray, Amen!

"If you constantly see no progress in life, then why not take some time and examine your behaviors, because progress often becomes difficult when you don't change the behaviors that might be limiting your progress"

#PrayerDrivenLife

Thursday

Seasonal Relationships

Seasonal people will come into your life; they act like friends, seem to be someone you can trust, and sometimes even feel like family, but they are just seasonal friends who will walk out of your life without any warning whatsoever. Whenever that happens, it's important not to get upset but to let them be who they are as they move on from you. We often allow ourselves to get so attached to people, which can blind us into false friendships and false relationships with people who have no value for anyone but themselves. Be very cautious about how you position your heart, and especially be careful with your conversations, even if it hurts your heart to see them move on from you, because sometimes, whether the connections you've had with people were good or bad, it's those types of connections and experiences, which might be preparing you, and strengthening you in ways you can never imagine. Life is always teaching us lessons, but the question is . . . Are you capitalizing on the wisdom you can learn from life's experiences?

Friday

SCRIPTURE:
1 John 4:8.
He who does not love does not know God, for God is love. In this the love of God was manifested toward us, that God has sent His only begotten Son into the world, that we might live through Him. In this is love, not that we loved God, but that He loved us and sent His Son to be the propitiation for our sins.

Love can truly be easy if we receive it in our hearts. Love conquers all things. It neutralizes behaviors in ways that positions one to be kind, even at times when their patience is tested most . . .

Lord Jesus, thank You for the sacrifices You made for us. Thank You for all the examples You taught us to show love and compassion towards others. It is my desire to always love just as You have instructed us to do towards others, and to always strive to be patience with others. This is something I cannot do, without the presence of Your love in my heart. Amen!!
1 John 4:8.

Saturday

Facing My Inner Truths

My greatest weakness throughout my life was hearing the truth about myself. I was comfortable with you as long as you were comfortable with who I am, but sometimes, we need someone who loves us enough to tell us the truth. Someone who isn't afraid to provoke change when we don't see a need to change within ourselves. Sometimes, seeing yourself without looking in the mirror is difficult. It's easier to see your flaws when you're open-minded to corrections. I'm constantly thanking God daily for positioning my heart to listen without "rejected hearing." Wisdom has taught me to absorb "effective criticism" and use it to change my life when necessary. Refrain from rejecting change or self-improvement. Learn to analyze and critique yourself, and most importantly, learn to face reality and realize that we are all a work in progress, but with God's help and guidance, victory will surely be the outcome.

Sunday

SCRIPTURE:
Isaiah 55:11
So shall My word be that goes forth from My mouth; It shall not return to Me void, But it shall accomplish what I please, And it shall prosper in the thing for which I sent it.

Heavenly Father, today I speak life over my surroundings, I pray for wisdom to navigate throughout this day. I pray for healing and strength, even as my body is slow to move, I pray for a mindset that empowers, and rejuvenates my health, as well as a mind that's ready to take on the challenges of this day. Help me Father God, to keep love in my heart, to always appreciate life at every level no matter the circumstances. Keep me humble without boasting, and prepare me today to be used in mighty ways according to Your will. In Jesus name I pray, not only for myself, but for everyone who reads this prayer today that Healing, Prosperity, and Peace shall be upon your life throughout this day. Amen

Final Words

Thank you for taking this journey to read my new book, PRAYER DRIVEN LIFE. I'm grateful for your support and pray that this book's contents will continue to bless your life for many years. I hope this book empowers you to live a troubled free, fulfilling life. Prayer gives us so much hope; it keeps us connected to God and is our lifeline which builds our faith in trusting God no matter how challenging life becomes. Even though I wrote this book and spent many months reading it to edit it, it continues to be a helpful resource for me, a pillar that leads me to prayer, and it inspires me with hope and peace. This lifelong journey that we all must travel is less complicated than we often live, but we usually make life difficult due to a lack of preparation. We should never allow life to overwhelm us, but instead, we must always be prepared to conquer life, and what better way to conquer life than through the power of God's word and our relationship with Him?

In closing, I leave you with this challenge. I challenge you and encourage you to pray often, seek God through prayer, and develop the consistency you need to be consistent in your relationship with Him. As you become more consistent, you will see amazing things happening. It will give you the confidence to take on the challenges of living in this world. It will strengthen your faith as well as your relationship with God. This is my challenge to you, and most importantly, it's my desire and hope that you shall succeed. God bless you and thank you for your support!

rolandgaskin.com's
STEP UP

Your Knowledge With Training!

This Course Includes:

Technology In Ministry | Building A Media Team

Social Media | Photography In Ministry | Web Design

Account Management | Security Plus More . . .

I am ready to provide you with On-location training for workshops, Ministry conferences, and seminars.

Visit: www.rolandgaskin.com

Dedication

I dedicated this book to the following people who have impacted my life over the the years. I genuinely miss each of them, and although they are no longer with us, memories of them will always be enbedded in my heart forever . . .

My Grandmother : Lucille Gaskin
My Mother: Luvonne Gaskin
Great Grandmother and Grandfather: Cornelius and Sadie Anderson
Father: Johnny B Battle
Oldest Brother: Willie James Mobley
My Two Aunts: Dorthy Coney, and Lenora Florence.
My God Parents Rev. Robert and Roxie Kinney
Uncle and Aunt: Carnelius Bo Anderson, and Ruth Anderson

And all other relatives and friends who are no longer with us. Thank you for the memories.

This book contains Scripture taken from the New King James Version®. Copyright © 1982 by Thomas Nelson. Used by permission. All rights reserved.

www.ingramcontent.com/pod-product-compliance
Lightning Source LLC
Chambersburg PA
CBHW051525230426
43668CB00012B/1739